HOW TO SPEND $50 BILLION TO MAKE THE WORLD
A BETTER PLACE

In a world fraught with problems and challenges, we need to gauge how to achieve the greatest good with our money. This unique publication provides a rich set of dialogs examining the most serious challenges facing the world today:

- climate change
- communicable diseases
- conflicts and arms proliferation
- access to education
- governance and corruption
- malnutrition and hunger
- migration
- sanitation and access to clean water
- subsidies and trade barriers.

Each problem is introduced by a world-renowned expert who defines the scale of the problem and examines a range of policy options. Shorter pieces offer alternative positions.

This abridged version of the highly lauded *Global Crises, Global Solutions* provides a serious yet accessible springboard for debate and discussion on the world's most serious problems and what we can do to solve them.

Bjørn Lomborg is Adjunct Professor in the Department of Management, Politics, and Philosophy at the Copenhagen Business School. He is also the author of the controversial bestseller, *The Skeptical Environmentalist* (Cambridge, 2001).

ADVANCE PRAISE FOR *HOW TO SPEND $50 BILLION TO MAKE THE WORLD A BETTER PLACE*

"This is a stimulating intellectual game with important real-world consequences. Lomborg asks all of us to stop talking grandly and vaguely about solving global problems and instead to rank them – based not only on the potential harm they can cause but also on our ability to turn things around. To govern is to choose and this pithy book forces us to choose."

> – Fareed Zakaria, *Newsweek* columnist and author of *The Future of Freedom*

"The world's staggering problems won't be solved by singing pop songs, denouncing villains, or adopting the proper moral tone, but by figuring out which policies have the best chance of doing the most good. If the world is going to become a better place, it will be because of the kinds of thinking on display in this courageous and fascinating book."

> – Steven Pinker, Professor, Harvard University, and author of *How the Mind Works* and *The Blank Slate*

"This book helps you make up your own mind, prioritize, and make your own choice. It is highly topical and just in time."

> – Kevin Roberts, CEO Worldwide, Saatchi & Saatchi, and author of *Lovemarks: The Future Beyond Brands*

"Bjørn Lomborg and his economist colleagues have produced a fascinating and unexpected consensus, which can start a debate about global priorities: Should we prioritize a costly and uncertain attempt to reduce effects of global warming in a hundred years time while millions are dying for lack of mosquito nets or condoms?"

> – Matt Ridley, author of *Nature via Nurture*

How to Spend
$50 Billion
to Make the World
a Better Place

Edited by
Bjørn Lomborg
Copenhagen Business School

CAMBRIDGE UNIVERSITY PRESS
Cambridge, New York, Melbourne, Madrid, Cape Town, Singapore, São Paulo

Cambridge University Press
32 Avenue of the Americas, New York, NY 10013-2473, USA

www.cambridge.org
Information on this title: www.cambridge.org/9780521866798

First published 2006

Printed in the United States of America

A catalog record for this publication is available from the British Library.

Library of Congress Cataloging in Publication Data

How to spend $50 billion to make the world a better place / edited by Bjørn
Lomborg.
    p.   cm.
An abridged edition of: Global crises, global solutions / edited by Bjørn
Lomborg. 2004.
Includes bibliographical references and index.
ISBN-13: 978-0-521-86679-8 (hardback)
ISBN-10: 0-521-86679-0 (hardback)
ISBN-13: 978-0-521-68571-9 (pbk.)
ISBN-10: 0-521-68571-0 (pbk.)
1. International cooperation.   2. Globalization.   3. Economic development.
4. Economic policy.   5. Economic development – Environmental aspects.
I. Lomborg, Bjørn, 1965–   II. Global crises, global solutions.   III. Title.
JZ1318.G55662   2006
361.2′6 – dc22   2006009560

ISBN-13   978-0-521-86679-8 hardback
ISBN-10   0-521-86679-0 hardback

ISBN-13   978-0-521-68571-9 paperback
ISBN-10   0-521-68571-0 paperback

Contents

Contributors

Chapter Authors

Harold Alderman is Lead Human Development Economist in the Africa Region of the World Bank, Washington, DC.

Kym Anderson is Lead Economist in the International Trade Unit of the World Bank's Development Research Group.

Jere R. Behrman is William R. Kenan, Jr., Professor in Economics and Director, Population Studies Center, University of Pennsylvania.

William R. Cline is Senior Fellow, Institute for International Economics and the Center for Global Development in Washington, DC.

Paul Collier is Professor and Director of the Centre for the Study of African Economies, Oxford University.

John Hoddinott is Senior Research Fellow in the Food Consumption and Nutrition Division of the International Food Policy Research Institute, Washington, DC.

Anke Hoeffler is Research Associate of the Centre for the Study of African Economies, Oxford University.

Philip Martin is Professor and Chair, UC Comparative Immigration and Integration Program, University of California, Davis.

Anne Mills is Professor of Health Economics and Policy, London School of Hygiene & Tropical Medicine.

Lant Pritchett is Lead Economist of the Environment and Social Unit at the World Bank.

Frank Rijsberman is Director General, International Water Management Institute, Colombo, Sri Lanka; Professor at UNESCO-IHE, International Institute for Water Education, Delft, and Wageningen University and Research, Wageningen.

Susan Rose-Ackerman is Henry R. Luce Professor of Jurisprudence, Yale University, Law School and Department of Political Science.

Sam Shillcutt is Research Fellow in the Health Economics and Financing Programme, London School of Hygiene and Tropical Medicine.

Perspective Paper Authors

Tony Addison is Professor, Deputy Director, Project Director and Senior Research Fellow, World Institute for Development Economics Research (WIDER) of the United Nations University (UNU).

Jens Christopher Andvig is Senior Researcher, University of Oslo.

Simon Appleton is Senior Lecturer in Economics, School of Economics, University of Nottingham.

Roger Böhning is Director, Programme on Promoting the Declaration on Fundamental Principles and Rights at Work, International Labour Office, Geneva.

John Boland is Professor Emeritus, Environmental Economics and Policy, Department of Geography and Environmental Engineering, The Johns Hopkins University.

Jean Cartier-Bresson is Professor of Economics, Université de Versailles, Saint-Quentin en Yvelines.

David Evans is Director, Department of Health System Financing, Expenditure and Resource Allocation (FER), World Health Organisation.

Michael Intriligator is Professor Emeritus of Economics, Political Science and Policy Studies, University of California, Los Angeles, and Senior Fellow, Milken Institute.

Alan Manne (1925–2005) was Professor Emeritus of Operations Research, Stanford University.

Robert Mendelsohn is Edwin Weyerhaeuser Davis Professor, Professor of Economics, and Professor in the School of Management, Yale University.

Arvind Panagaryia is Professor of Economics and Jagdish Bhagwati Professor of Indian Political Economy, Columbia University.

Jan Pronk is Professor of International Development Policy, Institute of Social Studies, University of Amsterdam.

Mark Rosenzweig is Mohamed Kamal Professor of Public Policy, at Kennedy School, Harvard University.

Paul Schultz is Malcolm K. Brachman Professor of Economics, Department of Economics, Yale University.

Peter Svedberg is Professor of Development Economics, The Institute for International Economic Studies, University of Stockholm.

Jacques van der Gaag is Professor of Development Economics, University of Amsterdam.

Ludger Wößmann is Head of the Department of Human Capital and Structural Change at the IFO Institute of Economic Research, University of Munich.

BJØRN LOMBORG[1]

Introduction
What Should We Do First?[2]

Each day decisions are made about global political priorities. We choose to support some worthy causes while others are disregarded. Unfortunately, political decisions seldom take into account a comprehensive view of the effects and costs of solving one problem in relation to another. Priorities are often set in an obfuscated environment involving the conflicting demands of the media, the people, and politicians. Despite all good intentions, the decision-making process is marred by arbitrary and haphazard methods. The idea behind the Copenhagen Consensus is to render, in the future, this process less arbitrary, because political decisions should not be made arbitrarily, but should be based on facts and knowledge. The result stemming from the Copenhagen Consensus 2004 is very concrete: a ranked list of real challenges, for real people, in the real world.

[1] Director, Copenhagen Consensus Center / Copenhagen Business School.
[2] Translated by Gitanjali Kapila.

If we had an extra $50 billion to put to good use, which problems would we solve first? That was the question put to the participants of the Copenhagen Consensus. Using more than 600 pages of scholarly papers as their point of departure, the participants engaged in an intense scholarly discussion that resulted in a set list of priorities regarding the world's most challenging problems.

This book constitutes a concrete contribution to the debate regarding global priorities – the question of how do we tackle the world's problems, such as where should we start, and what should be done. The text adumbrates some of the world's most pressing challenges, what can be done, how much it will cost, and what benefits will result. Armed with the information contained in these articles, readers will be in a better position to participate in the discussion of global priorities – and, in the spirit of the Copenhagen Consensus, to generate their own lists.

The articles stem from the international conference, the Copenhagen Consensus, held in Copenhagen from the 24th to the 28th of May 2004, where 38 economists threw themselves headlong into a debate – one that was both practical and theoretical – on how we can best solve the world's greatest problems.

The Copenhagen Consensus convened eight distinguished economists, each of whom prepared an economics paper on serious global problems, from hunger and clean drinking water to disease and climate change. These eight researchers came to Copenhagen and presented their results. Additionally, twenty prominent researchers, engaged to argue against these results, also were in attendance. The expert panel included eight top economists, among them four Nobel laureates, whose task it was to listen to all of the arguments, assess the ten areas of inquiry, and prioritize the solutions. This book contains summaries of the nine scholarly papers and rebuttals, all of which are written in language that is easy to understand.

Why were all the experts economists? Many have questioned this. The goal for the Copenhagen Consensus was to set priorities using the expertise of economists to set economic priorities. It seems clear that climate issues are best assessed by climate experts, and issues relating to malaria are best evaluated by malaria experts. If we asked a malaria expert or a climate expert to prioritize global warming or communicable diseases as the most pressing global concern, it would not be difficult to imagine which issue each would find most important. As such, economists were the featured experts at the Copenhagen Consensus.

The purpose of the Copenhagen Consensus was to build a bridge between the ivory tower of research and the general public. We need the rational calculations of economists in order to understand how we can best realize compassionate solutions that will make for a better world. Research should be utilized. Knowledge should be utilized. These facts were taken very seriously at the Copenhagen Consensus.

The task assigned to the expert panel was not easy. They found that in some areas the information that was available – upon which they were to base their evaluations – was inadequate. This applied to education, armed conflict, and financial instability. Another important result of the Copenhagen Consensus is that it is clear that there is a need for further research in these areas.

This process is somewhat similar to the one being used by the UN's Intergovernmental Panel on Climate Change. When the Panel first issued its report on the consequences of discharging greenhouse gases, it was evident that the report lacked critical information. This finding led to new research. When the Panel issued its second and third reports, many of the original lacunas in the first report were addressed. This process resulted in creating a better foundation for the decision-making process.

That the task before us is difficult ought not to deter us from attempting it. That we don't know everything should not keep us from using what we do know. The material available to the participants of the Copenhagen Consensus indicates that a fairly comprehensive knowledge base exists about a host of issues and their possible solutions.

The top economists who participated in the Copenhagen Consensus exhibited a certain modesty vis-à-vis the difficult task before them. I want to emphasize that the expert panel was not bound in any way. The eight economists made all decisions, of course – and this, in itself, could be considered the crowning achievement of the Copenhagen Consensus. However, what is perhaps most surprising is that they *were* able to come to a consensus. The eight came to a surprising amount of agreement. The Experts Panel Ranking chapter details the decisions at which the expert panel arrived. And the encouraging news from this unanimous panel is that something *can* be done – that there are good opportunities for investment to be made to improve conditions for the billions of poor in the world.

The expert panel at the Copenhagen Consensus agreed that first and foremost the world ought to concentrate on controlling HIV/AIDS. At a cost of $27 billion, around 28 million cases of the illness could be prevented by 2010. The benefit-cost ratio is predicted to be 40 times that figure. The HIV/AIDS crisis provides an excellent example of how fighting disease is a good investment.

Malnutrition and hunger are number two on the expert panel's list. Diseases that are a result of iron-, zinc-, iodine-, and A-vitamin deficiencies can be alleviated with subsidies. The benefits in relation to the cost outlay would be enormous. The expert panel recommends that an investment of $12 billion be made to address this problem. Today more than two billion people are iron-deficient. The importance of alleviating malnutrition and hunger, especially among children, cannot be overestimated.

Trade liberalization is number three on the list. The costs of introducing trade reform would be very modest. The benefits, however, would be enormous, up to $2,400 billion per year.

The elimination of trade barriers does not require a large monetary investment. However, political willingness is of utmost importance. Rich and poor countries alike would benefit from free trade, and greater prosperity means that there will be greater resources to solve more of the world's serious problems.

Ranked fourth on the expert panel's list was the control and treatment of malaria. Mosquito nets treated with insect repellent was proposed as an investment that would yield high returns.

Aside from the treatment of disease, hunger, and free trade, initiatives to ensure clean drinking water and better governance were also high on the list.

The experts have answered the question: If we had an additional $50 billion available to improve the world, where should we invest first? A unanimous panel of top economists recommends that $27 billion be used to fight HIV/AIDS, $12 billion for malnutrition and hunger, that the reduction of trade barriers, whose costs would be modest, be initiated, and that $10 billion be used to fight malaria.

The point of departure for the Copenhagen Consensus is that the world is plagued with a plethora of problems and we don't have the resources to solve them all here and now. The good news from the expert panel is that appropriate solutions can be found. HIV/AIDS, malnutrition, trade barriers, and malaria are all problems that can be effectively solved.

Topping the list of priorities set by the expert panel are basic problems that affect billions of people worldwide. New technology, economic growth, and development have improved living conditions for many people. Nevertheless, there remains the pressing – and basic – need for an adequate and predictable food supply and the expectation of good health.

So much for challenges that can be solved. Both experts and those with good intentions are quick to agree that solutions should be initiated. Were we not already aware that fighting disease and malnutrition are worthy causes? Who would disagree? But now, the economists tell us that it is an economically sound idea to invest in the future of humanity.

What about the rest of the list? The bad solutions? It is not only difficult to set priorities – it is also unpleasant. The ranking of problems doesn't only imply that one problem stands at the top, but also that one lies at the bottom. This way of thinking is anathema to many. Shouldn't we just do everything? Solve hunger, stop climate change, prevent war, etc.? Isn't it irresponsible to rank one problem above another?

Making choices implies leaving something out. The experts divided their lists into four categories: very good projects; good projects; fair projects; and bad projects. In the bad projects category they placed a proposal regarding migration and one for guest-worker programs for the unskilled. Also, there were three proposals relating to climate change that stood at the bottom. These included the Kyoto Protocol and various proposals regarding the taxation of carbon dioxide discharge.

The experts are not unaware that climate change is important. But, for some of the world's poorest countries, which will be adversely affected by climate change, problems like HIV/AIDS, hunger, and malaria are more pressing and can be solved with more efficacy. Expert panel member Professor Stokey stressed that climate change is a serious problem, but that the proposals made, including Kyoto, are not very effective. There is a need for more research in this area.

Some critics believe that the methods used by the Copenhagen Consensus were, all in all, much too myopic in focusing on economic costs and benefits. Yet two other prioritizations made by non-economists seem to support the economists' choices. First, it is interesting to note that the ranking of issues by the top economists closely resembled the results of 80 young students who were given the same task as the experts. Christian Friis Bach stresses that though the participants of the Youth Forum chose other solutions for the problems cited, the list of priorities they set quite closely resembled the one drafted by the experts. In addition, he describes the way in which the Youth Forum participants often suggested far-sighted solutions, and that these were perhaps better. It is true that the choice lies between clinics and condoms, but the difficult question still remains: Should we save 1,000,000 lives with condoms or 100,000 with a comparable cost outlay for clinics? Second, the Danish newspaper, *Politiken*, also asked a small expert panel in Uganda to prioritize the formidable challenges facing humanity and the result was amazingly similar to the ranking of the economists. Thus, quite a bit of evidence exists that indicates that there is widespread support for the priorities set by the economists.

This fact – that the cold, rational overview of the economists, the enthusiastic discussions of the Copenhagen Youth Forum, and an Ugandan panel – essentially came to the same set of conclusions confirms that disease and hunger are urgent problems.

The Copenhagen Consensus has also been criticized for comparing apples and oranges. How can one set priorities among problems such as hunger and climate change when they are so vastly different in kind? Sure, it's difficult. But it is precisely these kinds of decisions that politicians make each day. Priorities are set when the choice is made to build a traffic circle to ensure traffic safety over funding home help for seniors, or between new schools and better hospitals. And the setting of priorities doesn't disappear if they are not discussed – the decision-making process behind them simply becomes less visible. For this reason the discussion regarding the setting of priorities is relevant.

The Copenhagen Consensus has also been criticized for assuming from the outset that there is not enough money for everything. Will the conclusions reached at the Copenhagen Consensus be leveraged to rationalize budget cuts? It is my belief that we will see the opposite effect. The Copenhagen Consensus will create an increased awareness of the problems we face and thus generate more investment in developing nations. Simply put: We show that money can improve the world.

Some have questioned the whole idea behind the Copenhagen Consensus – the very necessity of creating priorities.

Just think – what if doctors did not perform triage? If doctors working in an emergency room didn't prioritize the treatment of patients based on the seriousness of their illnesses? What if doctors simply treated those who by chance stood first in line or complained the loudest? A broken arm could be treated before a heart attack. This approach would cost lives and result in a misguided use of resources. As such, it would never be considered. Should we thus consider using this method when considering how to alleviate the problems of the world's poorest people?

Those who will not acknowledge that resources are limited live in a dream world. At the risk of being offensive, I believe that the world has more need for realists than for dreamers. It's very easy to want to support all good causes, but in the real world this is just not possible.

Do dreamers – with all their good intentions – have a monopoly on being good? Are the priorities of realists misguided?

Measured by the effect on those who suffer most in the world I am inclined to re-think the relationship between dreamers and the realists. It is unethical not to take into account knowledge that indicates where we can do the most good. The Copenhagen Consensus constitutes the cold, rational approach. Instead of intending to do good, isn't it better to actually *do* good?

The Copenhagen Consensus has shown that an informed ranking of priorities is possible, and that economic cost-benefit analyses do not lead to short-sighted solutions or a fixation on money. On the contrary, they lead to a focus on the problems of people living in impoverished conditions.

I'm proud that we have realized the first goal of the Copenhagen Consensus, namely a list of priorities regarding the world's most challenging problems. Experts have used their knowledge and insight to commit themselves to create a set of concrete solutions. The Copenhagen Consensus has already initiated an important debate on the prioritization of the world's resources.

The Copenhagen Consensus is conceived as a concrete resource for politicians. But will they use it? My hope has always been that when the list first became available, it would be impossible to ignore – because it's based on knowledge, and because it's so concrete.

But the Copenhagen Consensus shouldn't only concern politicians. It's important that the rest of us also become involved in the discussion of priorities, that we consider the facts, and that we face the difficult but inevitable task of having to choose among a long list of important issues. This book offers readers the opportunity to exploit the best research in order to improve the debate, to come up with their own informed lists. The next goal for the Copenhagen Consensus is to involve both academics and politicians in the debate. I hope very much that each of you will participate in this absolutely necessary discussion about global priorities – namely, what we should do first.

WILLIAM R. CLINE[1]

1 Meeting the Challenge of Global Warming

Introduction

This chapter compares the costs and benefits of three alternative policy strategies to reduce mankind's emissions of greenhouse gases and limit damage due to global warming.

It is particularly difficult to analyze the economics of policies to limit such emissions because expected benefits to be generated from such policy actions will materialize only in the distant future, whereas many of the costs will be incurred much sooner. Therefore the way in which future benefits are discounted to give a present value is crucial: How much is the prospect of $100 earned in 50 or 100 years worth to us today? This is discussed below in more detail before the model used for evaluating the three policy options is described.

[1] Center for Global Development and Institute for International Economics.

The state of global warming science and policy

The Intergovernmental Panel on Climate Change (IPCC) provides a framework for scientists from across the world to share and evaluate the data generated by a range of computer models projecting future changes to atmospheric composition, average temperatures, and climate patterns. The IPCC periodically reviews this situation, most recently in the Third Assessment Report (TAR) published in 2001. This report compiles a vast amount of detailed scientific information, which is distilled into a "Summary for Policy-makers" agreed to by all participating governments. This summary is the basis for planning future action.

The TAR projects an increase in average temperatures by 2100 in the range 1.4–5.8°C (above the 1990 baseline). It is also estimated that global average surface temperature rose by 0.6°C from 1861 to 2000, and the panel concluded that "most of the observed warming over the last 50 years is likely to have been due to the increase in greenhouse gas concentrations." Of the six recognized greenhouse gases, carbon dioxide (CO_2) plays the greatest role because it is emitted in the greatest quantities and persists for long periods in the atmosphere.

When projecting future temperature rises, the climate models use a range of six benchmark scenarios, which give rise to very different patterns of man-made carbon dioxide emissions. It is implicitly assumed in the TAR that all these scenarios have equal weight, and therefore that the future temperature rise is equally likely to be anywhere within the projected range. However, the analysis in this

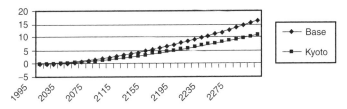

Figure 1.1. Climate damage as percent of GWP, baseline, and Kyoto Protocol

chapter assumes that some scenarios that predict low emissions are extremely unlikely without economic incentives, which means that future temperature rise would be towards the upper end of the range.

International policy on mitigation of climate change is focused on the Kyoto Protocol negotiated in 1997. This treaty sets limits on emissions of carbon dioxide allowed from industrialized and transition economies without making any demands on the developing world. This agreement was seen as the first, relatively small, step by the international community in a more ambitious, long-term program of emissions reduction. However, there now seems little chance of the Kyoto Protocol coming into force globally. The USA has made clear that it will not ratify the treaty, both because of the economic harm it would cause and the uncertainty surrounding climate science. Russia seems unlikely to ratify, for similar reasons.

The Protocol must be ratified by industrialized and transition countries, accounting for at least 55% of total emissions, to come into force. Without Russia's ratification, this cannot be achieved. Although some signatories, particularly

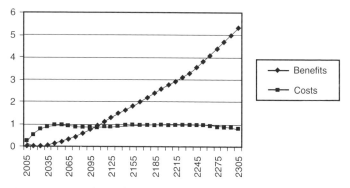

Figure 1.2. Benefits and costs of Kyoto Protocol abatement (% world product)

EU countries, have their own programs to limit emissions, few are meeting their self-imposed targets.

The Kyoto Protocol is discussed further below as one of the policy options. However, it is now doubtful that the Protocol is still relevant because of lack of support from key players. A more likely option is the re-opening of international negotiations to arrive at a new agreement to be supported by the United States, Russia, and developing countries.

Core analytical issues

For most projects, the economic analysis on which decisions are based covers a period of, at most, a few decades. However, global warming takes place on a much longer timescale. IPCC projections cover at least the period up to 2100. But arguably, the proper time horizon is in fact 300 years, because it would take that long for carbon dioxide to be mixed into the deep ocean and so start to reverse its build-up in the atmosphere.

Conventional discounting, even with low discount rates, makes present day values of benefits to be received far in the future vanishingly small. The reason why we discount the value of expected future benefits is that people tend to prefer consumption sooner rather than later. If asked to choose between getting $100 today or $100 in a year's time, most people would prefer $100 now. When people save money, they forestall consumption today. Generally, they are only willing to do that because the savings can be invested to yield an interest premium that ensures future consumption will be larger. (Taking account of the large costs involved in the short term, a conventional economic analysis would nearly always strongly suggest that no action be taken. And yet, potentially severe climate damage can only be limited by taking costly actions now. How can we establish an economic case for such actions?)

As an alternative to the conventional method, a system of "utility-based discounting" is proposed. This approach is used in the economics literature on social cost-benefit analysis. In this case, the discount rate for "pure time preference" (explicit preference for consumption today over consumption tomorrow) is set at zero. However, future consumption is still discounted on the basis that per capita consumption will increase, so the marginal benefit of extra consumption will fall (for example, buying a car has an enormous benefit compared to not having one at all; buying a second car for convenience has a smaller additional benefit). In this case, the discount rate applied is called the

Social Rate of Time Preference (SRTP). Because the long-term per capita growth rate is about 1%, and because extra utility from extra consumption is estimated to decline by 1.5% when consumption per capita rises by 1%, the effective total discount rate is about 1.5%. This equals zero for the component of "pure" time preference (or "impatience") and 1.5% for the component reflecting falling "marginal utility."

Although there has been considerable work on the costs of mitigating global warming, calculations of the benefits (the climate-induced damage avoided) are far more difficult to make. Based on figures available in the early 1990s, the potential damage calculated for a doubling of atmospheric CO_2 would amount to some 1% GDP annually, with one-quarter of this related to agriculture. Other authors have come to similar conclusions, with rates of damage skewed toward developing countries because of their reduced scope for adaptation.

Some economists have also tried to include an allowance for potential catastrophic change in their assessments. A number of possible catastrophes have been postulated, including the widely publicized shut-down of the so-called thermohaline circulation in the Atlantic Ocean.

It has been suggested that the present "conveyor belt," in which cold water sinking in the Arctic induces upwelling of warm water in the southern Atlantic, could stop as melting polar ice makes Arctic waters less salty. In Northwestern Europe, this circulation pattern manifests itself as the Gulf Stream, a phenomenon believed to have a significant moderating effect on the regional climate. It has been calculated that the economic loss for Europe of such a catastrophic shutdown could be over 40% of GDP. The probability of such an occurrence rises steeply with the extent of global temperature rise, leading to the conclusion that, in the case of a 6°C rise, the potential costs would warrant Europe sacrificing 10% of GDP to avoid the catastrophe.

Previous cost–benefit analyses

In earlier work by the present author, it was assumed that, in the absence of policy changes, emissions of greenhouse gasses would continue to rise to a maximum of 50 GtC (gigatonnes, or million million tons of carbon) in the latter part of the 23rd century, from a baseline of 6.9 GtC in 2000. This was based on the assumption that the large known reserves of coal would increasingly be exploited as oil and gas reserves are depleted.

A central value of 10°C for temperature rise by 2300 was estimated, giving an annual cost of 16% of global GDP. Abatement costs are also difficult to estimate, but making reasonable assumptions about the availability of alternative energy sources and the application of today's best technology, it would cost around 2% of the global economic product to cut world emissions in half by 2050. Because of the development of further technological alternatives, this same cost could produce a net emission reduction of 80% by the end of the 21st century.

An alternative model (DICE) has been used for the past two decades by William Nordhaus to estimate optimal carbon abatement. His most recent studies have indicated an optimum of rather modest reductions in carbon emissions

(5% at present, 11% by 2100), mediated by a carbon tax of $9 per tons by 2005, rising to $67 per tons by the end of the century. The result would be a reduction in warming of less than 0.1°C.

It is not the abatement costs as such that lead to such limited results: In fact, figures generated for 2045 suggest that it would cost only 0.03% of global GDP to reduce emissions by 10% (double what the model identifies as optimal) and less than 1% to halve them. The results are driven by the calculated low present value of the benefit, in turn determined by conventional assumptions about time discounting.

The proposals in this chapter are therefore based on an adapted version of this model – considered a good one for showing the effects of policies over time – but using the preferred Social Rate of Time Preference (SRTP) discounting approach.

Adapting the DICE99 model

The main changes made to this model (called DICE99CL in its modified form) are:

- Setting pure time preference (the conventional discount rate) at zero.
- Discounting future consumption using the SRTP approach. This implies a falling marginal value of consumption with growth.
- Shadow-pricing capital. The social cost–benefit approach converts capital into consumption equivalents, taking account of the fact that a proportion of the

abatement costs would come from investment rather than consumption.

- Increasing baseline carbon emissions. In Nordhaus' recent use of the DICE model, he assumes a significant reduction in carbon intensity (tons of carbon per unit of GDP) by the end of the century because of large increases in extraction costs for fossil fuels. This is not consistent with other analysts' views on future emission scenarios, so the adapted model reflects what the present author considers to be the more realistic of the IPCC scenarios.

The net effect of these and other changes is to raise the warming baseline, although it is still somewhat more optimistic than several of the IPCC scenarios. In the adapted model, warming reaches 3.3°C by 2100, 5.5°C by 2200, and 7.3°C by 2300.

Alternative policy strategies

The adapted model examined above is applied to the analysis of the following three policy options. Note that adaptation to climate change is not considered to be a credible separate option. Rather, it is assumed that for all three policies feasible adaptations are already undertaken as part of the baseline case.

Option 1: Optimal carbon tax

This policy is for an internationally agreed and coordinated tax to be levied by national governments. Each country would use the proceeds for its own purposes.

Optimal emission cuts (based on 1990 emissions as the baseline) would start at around the 40% mark, rise to nearly 50% by the end of the century, and peak at 63% in 2200 before declining to around 15% in 2300. Carbon taxes to achieve this would be similarly aggressive: $170 per ton in 2005, $600 in 2100, peaking at $1,300 in 2200, and tapering off.

The net effect is a gradual widening of the gap between projected warming from "business as usual" and the optimized carbon tax approach: By 2300, the temperature rise is limited to 5.4°C compared to the 7.3°C baseline. The discounted present value of the abatement costs is $128 trillion, but the value of benefits from avoiding damage is $271 trillion: a benefit-cost ratio of 2.1. Although this is what the model defines as optimal, there is still considerable scope to implement an even more aggressive tax policy and further reduce warming while still producing a benefit-cost ratio of more than one.

Option 2: The Kyoto Protocol

This option would commit the industrialized and transition economies to cutting emissions by 5% below 1990 levels and maintaining them at that level, with no constraints on developing economies. Such an approach would reduce global emissions far less than the Option 1.

Although the effect on temperature rise is modest – a reduction from 7.3° to 6.1° by 2300 – damage to the world economy is reduced from 15.4% to 10.3%. Over the same period, the benefits rise steadily after a lag period, becoming greater than costs around 2100, and reaching more than 5%

of global GDP by 2300. The present value of the benefits is $166 trillion, against costs of $94 trillion, which yields a benefit-cost ratio of 1.77.

However, assuming the Kyoto Protocol option is the only abatement strategy in place, the full costs are borne by the present industrialized and transition economies ('Annex 1' countries). For this, they receive benefits of only $55 trillion, making the Protocol an unattractive option for these countries in economic terms.

Option 3: A value-at-risk approach

Value-at-risk is a concept used to manage risk in the financial sector, which seeks to identify the maximum loss within specified confidence limits, usually 90% or more. With a 90% confidence limit, you can be 90% certain that you will not lose more than the calculated maximum loss. Amongst climatologists, this approach has been used to define an upper limit for the Climate Sensitivity parameter (CS), the equilibrium temperature rise following a doubling of atmospheric carbon dioxide level. Using all available data, it was calculated that there was a 95% probability of CS lying between 1.0 and 9.3°C. The value-at-risk approach then requires the evaluation of the damage caused when CS is at the upper end of the range (9.3°C); over twice the upper bound benchmark of 4.5°C used by the IPCC).

Using this higher figure in the climate model, instead of the mean IPCC CS value of 2.9°C, a new set of optimal abatement results is obtained. The baseline warming reaches 15°C by 2300, but this can be reduced to 5.9°C using optimal measures to reduce emissions. Reduction by 90%

is optimal (the model has this as an upper boundary) from now until the late 23rd century. To achieve this, a carbon tax starting at $450 per ton in 2005 would rise to $1,900 per ton in 2205, then decline after 2285.

Baseline climate-related damage would be massive: 8.6% of global GDP by 2100 and as high as 68% by 2300. Optimal reduction of emissions would reduce these figures to 2.1% and 9.4% respectively. Abatement costs average about 3.5% of global GDP through this century, plateauing at about 5% thereafter. The present value of the abatement costs is $458 trillion, but this is set against a benefit (damage avoided) of $1,749 trillion, which yields a benefit-cost ratio of 3.8. Therefore, although the taxes appear punitive, this scenario would be highly beneficial in net terms.

All these policies have been evaluated on the basis of zero pure time preference, as discussed earlier. If conventional time-based discounting is applied, even at low rates, the options would look rather different. For example, costs exceed benefits for Option 1 if the discount rate exceeds 1%, and for the third option, the policy ceases to be cost effective at a rate between 1 and 2%. Because the total discount rate is about 1.5% per year higher than the pure time preference rate, these breakeven points correspond to about 2.5% for the first option and about 3% for the third.

Conclusion

Three alternative policy options have been evaluated, using an adapted climate model that makes allowance for the long timescale over which benefits of emission abatement are received. The timescale for assessment is also extended through to the year 2300, a period over which the full impact of policies will be felt.

A fairly aggressive abatement policy – with carbon taxes set internationally but collected and spent nationally – is the basis of the first option. Global warming would be reduced by 0.8°C by 2100 and by 1.9°C by 2300, and the benefit-cost ratio would be approximately two, using the optimal solution.

The second option – following the Kyoto Protocol – would have more limited effects, although the benefits would still marginally outweigh the costs. However, all these costs would be borne by the present industrialized and transition economies.

The third option is based on an estimate of the maximum value-at-risk. This is a very risk-averse approach and would require a carbon tax of $450 per ton, rising to $1,900 by 2205, to cut carbon emissions by 90%. Despite the high cost of this option, its benefit-cost ratio is still about four.

CLIMATE CHANGE
OPPONENTS' VIEWS

In his challenge paper, William Cline paints a picture of severe long-term economic damage that would result from climate change if mankind does not take decisive action to reduce greenhouse gas emissions in the near future. His preferred option is the introduction of aggressive carbon taxes which would rise steadily over the next two to 300 years. Robert Mendlesohn, in his opposition paper, takes issue with the logic and analysis that leads Cline to these conclusions.

In Mendlesohn's view, Cline makes the mistake of proposing very costly (and economically damaging) strategies in the short term to tackle potential problems that might result from the action of future generations. He thinks it would be fairer for those costs to be borne by those generations causing the problem, if they so choose.

Economists use a process called discounting to compare costs and benefits over time. This accounts for the common-sense fact that it is only worthwhile spending money now if it produces future benefits greater than the interest which could be gained by saving it. Because Cline believes that climate damage in the far future is so important, he sets an artificially low discount rate so that the cost of damage appears large in present-day terms.

Another flaw is his reliance on older studies for estimates. More recently, there is systematic evidence from the literature that likely climate damage had previously been overestimated, since studies had failed to allow for adaptation and climate benefits. For example, countries in the polar regions would receive large benefits from warming, those in mid-latitudes would benefit as long as the average temperature rise was less than 2.5°C, and only tropical and sub-tropical regions would suffer short-term harm to the degree previously suggested. Overall, benefits of global warming are likely to outweigh damage until the rise is greater than 2.5°C, and even then the net damage would be far smaller than originally thought.

Such reduced impacts imply that fossil fuel use would not need to be cut as drastically as Cline suggests, and that carbon taxes should be much lower. These would start at only $1–2 per ton, rising to $10–20 per ton by 2100. This does not take account of the concerns about potentially catastrophic events such as shutting down the thermohaline circulation in the Atlantic, but Mendelsohn believes it is unrealistic to link current emissions to such hypothetical events.

He also argues that emissions of greenhouse gases should be controlled in the same way as any other pollutant: by the use of tradable permits. Companies can be issued with permits to emit a certain amount of carbon dioxide; if they release less, they can sell part of their allowance. A further major abatement policy that Cline does not cover is carbon sequestration: removal of carbon dioxide from the atmosphere, for example, by growing trees. Mendlesohn believes that an optimal forest management program can be constructed that could account for one-third of the total abatement. This would reduce the level of emissions tax needed.

Based on the more recent evidence, none of the options proposed by Cline would be cost-effective, in Mendlesohn's view: Only the much more modest proposals of carbon tax rates between $1 and $20 per ton for the next century have a benefit-cost ratio greater than one. In contrast, Cline's "optimal" program would yield a benefit-cost ratio of only 0.07 by 2100: $100 of cost would produce only $7 of benefit.

In summary, Mendlesohn argues for a much less draconian approach to climate change policy, and takes a far more optimistic view of mankind's ability to learn, adapt, and find better solutions. He proposes that commitments should only be made for what is definitely intended to be done in the near term, and that the policy should then be reviewed every decade in the light of new evidence.

Alan Manne, in his opposition paper, also agrees that Cline has overstated the immediacy of the problems presented by climate change. In his view, dealing with poverty and disease in developing countries warrants much higher priority. He criticizes Cline's arguments for an optimal carbon tax. He also objects to Cline considering an even more risk-averse solution (the so-called "value-at-risk" approach) that appears to justify yet higher carbon taxes. This is based on a highly pessimistic view of current uncertainties, many of which will be resolved in the future.

Manne's main concern, which he shares with Mendlesohn, is that Cline's discounting strategy is unduly alarmist. He uses an unrealistic economic analysis to achieve the result he wants.

Unlike Mendlesohn, Manne includes in his analysis factors such as impact on human health, species loss, and catastrophic risks such as shut-down of the Atlantic thermohaline circulation (so-called non-market damage). Indeed, in his view the market damages (losses to agriculture and fisheries, for example) that are the usual basis of economic analysis are not the principal reason to be concerned about climate change. How much individual countries would be prepared to pay to avoid climate damage depends on a number of factors, but will depend largely on the estimated benefit-cost ratio.

In Manne's opinion, Cline's use of an unrealistically low discount rate inevitably means that high carbon taxes, designed to force a rapid reduction in the use of fossil fuels, is the only reason this aggressive approach appears to be cost-effective.

A more measured, market oriented strategy would still limit temperature rise to 2.5°C, but would delay costly abatement measures, which a more prosperous future world might show a greater willingness to pay. In contrast to Cline's aggressive carbon tax rates, starting at $300 per ton, Manne's approach suggests a near-term optimal tax of $12 per ton. This is higher than Mendelsohn's $1–2 per ton, but nevertheless these two very different approaches still come to essentially the same conclusion: Cline's highly expensive, social engineering approach is not justified. Both authors put far more faith in mankind's ability to adapt and develop appropriately flexible solutions.

ANNE MILLS AND SAM SHILLCUTT[1]

2 Communicable Diseases

The challenge of communicable disease

The second half of the twentieth century saw enormous improvements in health across the whole world. Indeed, life expectancy in developing countries has increased faster than in the industrialized world, albeit from a lower baseline. People in many developing countries have life expectancies close to those in more advanced economies, but there is now a big gap between them and another group of countries, mainly in sub-Saharan Africa (SSA), where high mortality persists.

In 2002, there were 57 million deaths worldwide. Of these, 20% were children under five, and 98% of these childhood deaths occurred in developing countries. Communicable diseases represent seven out of the top 10 causes of child deaths in developing countries, and account for around 60% of all such deaths: more than 6 million deaths annually. A further problem in developing countries is premature

[1] Health Economics and Financing Programme, London School of Hygiene and Tropical Medicine.

mortality of adults (15–59), which represents 30% of all deaths, compared to only 20% in developed economies. As ever, it is the poorest in these countries who suffer disproportionately.

Non-smokers in the richest countries have a lower risk of dying throughout their life than other population categories. Deaths in excess of the rate in this category can be considered avoidable, and certain sectors of developing country societies, particularly infants and young women, are disproportionately affected. Around 90% of these avoidable deaths are caused by communicable diseases. The tools to tackle these have been employed to good effect in the world's richest countries, but the challenge is now to make them available to the world's poorest people.

In this chapter, the focus is on three major opportunities to combat communicable disease out of the many possibilities:

- Malaria control.
- HIV/AIDS control.
- Scaled-up basic health services.

Of course, these are to some extent interdependent, but we examine them separately for clarity.

Assessing the opportunities

Health has both direct and indirect effects on a country's economy; direct through the impact of ill health on current productivity, and indirect via the size and quality of the labor force as determined by such factors as

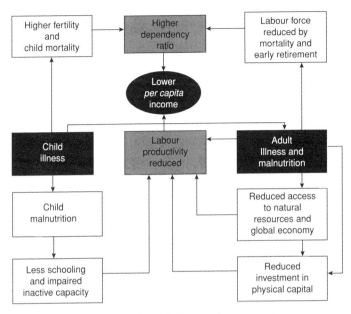

Figure 2.1. Channels through which illness reduces income
Source: Ruger, Jamison and Bloom (2001).

mortality, fertility, and intellectual capacity. The drain on economic performance through ill health can be reversed by appropriate interventions; for example, up to 1.7% of annual economic growth in East Asia between 1965 and 1990 (about half the total GDP increase for the period) has been attributed to massive improvements in public health. Some analysts even have argued that such health improvements have contributed at least as much to economic development as have innovation and expansion in goods and services.

The costs of poor health across communities can be assessed by both micro- and macroeconomic studies.

Microeconomic studies examine the effect of disease at a household level, but they tend to underestimate the full economic impact of poor health. This is partly because communities adopt coping mechanisms such as labor substitution within the family, liquidating assets, and increased birth-rates. Furthermore, because the state of health usually affects an entire community, there are no unaffected households with which to make direct comparisons, nor good ways of accurately assessing the value of alternative activities for which labor is unavailable.

Macroeconomic studies, in contrast, compare the effects of disease on the economies of different countries. Such studies attempt to capture the full, wide-ranging effects of ill health, but there is much less data of this type available.

Most studies of particular interventions have analyzed the data in terms of cost effectiveness rather than cost-benefit ratios, calculating the cost-per-life saved or disability averted. To draw on this data to produce a cost-benefit analysis, a monetary value must be placed on human life. This value will vary with the approach taken and assumptions made, introducing a degree of subjectivity into the final analysis.

In this chapter, these cost effectiveness studies and other relevant work have been used as a basis for calculating costs and benefits of the three opportunities being considered. No attempt has been made to extrapolate results for a particular country to a wider area, but the various pieces of evidence taken together give a sense of the overall cost-benefit balance. To avoid understating benefits, results are adjusted to Purchasing Power Parity and expressed in 2003 international dollars (Int $).

A standard discount rate of 3% has been used to calculate net present values. Simple sensitivity analyses were done to ensure the conclusions were not just valid for a single set of assumptions.

Control of malaria

Malaria – a parasitic disease spread by the Anopheles mosquito – is transmitted in 103 countries, and is estimated to cause 1–3 million deaths annually. It is now primarily a tropical disease, having been eradicated from North America, Europe, and Russia during the twentieth century.

Malaria is caused by four different species of the *Plasmodium* parasite. The most dangerous of these predominates in sub-Saharan Africa (SSA), where 90% of malarial deaths (and 85% of all infections) occur. There are two types of transmission:

1. **Stable**, in which young children are repeatedly infected. Those who survive acquire immunity, meaning that they are very unlikely to die from the disease as adults (although they may have recurrent fevers).
2. **Unstable**, where transmission rates are low and immunity does not develop. In this case, malaria epidemics occur, and deaths occur amongst all age groups.

In Africa, about 1 million deaths caused by malaria are believed to occur each year, more than three-quarters of them children. In SSA, malaria accounts for around 20%

of deaths of under-5s. This is a small proportion of the total disease burden: 200–450 million cases of malaria are estimated to occur among young children in Africa, and there could be in the region of 2 billion cases globally. 3% of attacks are characterized as severe, and half of those affected die if they do not receive hospital treatment.

In addition to the direct effects, malaria is an important cause of anemia, interacts with other infectious diseases, and contributes to Low Birth Weight when contracted during pregnancy. As well as its various direct and indirect physical effects, malaria is believed to have a significant negative impact on intellectual development.

Microeconomic impact

There is evidence of a considerable burden on households and governments for prevention and treatment. In Malawi, for example, it was estimated that the total annual direct cost of malaria for an average household was $40, representing over 7% of total income. Similar figures have been reported for small farmers in other African countries: 9–18% of income in Kenya, and 7–13% in Nigeria. It seems quite clear that the burden falls particularly heavily on the poorest in each society.

Direct evidence of the cost of strategies designed to cope with the *risk* of malaria is difficult to obtain, because they tend to apply to all households in a region. However, behavior such as maintaining a labor surplus to cope with illness in individuals can significantly reduce overall productivity.

Macroeconomic impact

A recent study suggests that the economies of countries with a large amount of malaria grew by 1.3% less per annum compared to unaffected countries in the period 1965–1990, resulting in an income level 33% lower than that of countries without malaria. A 10% reduction in malaria was associated with a 0.3% increase in annual growth.

Although others have found a quantitatively smaller effect, the result is still clear: In 1995, income levels in countries with endemic malaria were substantially lower than those without the disease.

Alleviation strategy

Good evidence on effectiveness is available only for individual interventions, not for a package, so this evaluation takes a package of measures that maximizes the number of people covered and minimizes overlap in order to avoid overestimation of benefits. The package includes use of insecticide-treated mosquito nets for children, a two-stage treatment of pregnant women in their first pregnancy. and a switch to a more effective drug combination for treatment of sufferers (with better coverage of those affected). This was evaluated for SSA, which carries by far the greatest burden of malaria.

Economic evaluation

Using macroeconomic data, the benefit-cost ratio was calculated for halving the malaria burden in sub-Saharan

Africa by 2015 (a target of the United Nations Millennium Project). The costs of reaching this goal are estimated at Int $21 per person per year. For the more than half a billion people at risk, the total cost would be Int $140 billion over the period 2002–2015. The benefits depend on which of two published models is used, but these lie between Int $275 billion and $660 billion over the same period. This gives a benefit-cost ratio of 1.9 or 4.7, and these ratios remain favorable even when assumptions of higher costs and discount rates are used.

The proposed intervention can also be assessed from a microeconomic standpoint. Considering each of the three components of the program for sub-Saharan Africa individually, over the Millennium Project timescale 2002–15:

- An increase in use of insecticide-treated mosquito nets by under-5s in SSA from the present estimated 2% to 70% would provide a benefit of nearly Int $18 billion annually, at a cost of Int $1.77 billion: a benefit-cost ratio of 10. An additional 60 million children would be protected in areas where malaria is endemic.
- Providing two-stage anti-malarial treatment to 90% of women in their first pregnancy would protect nearly 5 million mothers and their newborn infants annually. Over 2002–15, this would cost less than Int $0.5 billion and deliver benefits valued at Int $6.2 billion, an overall benefit-cost ratio of 12.1.
- Changing to the preferred artimisinin-based combination therapy (ACT) for malaria treatment (combined with dipstick screening to ensure treatment only of true

Table 2.1. Effects of HIV/AIDS on national GDP, 2000–2025

	2000 GDP ($m)	(%) loss no intervention	Monetary loss ($ m)
Algeria	186,900	36.20	67,658
Egypt	222,190	44.30	98,430
Iran	364,400	33.60	122,438
Jordan	18,684	27.90	5,213
Lebanon	17,950	26.30	4,721
Morocco	97,991	33.20	32,533
Tunisia	58,574	45.50	26,651
Yemen	13,954	31.40	4,382

Source: Calculated from Robalino, Jenkins and El Maroufi (2002).

malaria cases) for the 168 million people who are currently treated with less effective drugs would be highly beneficial. The benefit-cost ratio would be 38.6, with costs of Int $6.5 billion delivering benefits of Int $251 billion over the 2002–15 period. However, to meet the goal of halving malaria incidence, an additional 112 million cases would need to be treated each year. The incremental costs for this would be higher (Int $8.2 billion) but this treatment would deliver additional benefits of Int $158 billion, giving a benefit–cost ratio of 19.1.

Combining all these interventions, at an annual cost of just under Int $3 billion, would deliver some Int $50 billion in annual benefits over the Millennium Project timescale.

Control of HIV/AIDS

Although a global problem, more than 90% of HIV infections occur in developing countries. AIDS is responsible for over 5% of all deaths worldwide, accounting for between 2.5 and 3.5 million deaths in 2003. 5.3 million new infections occur each year. The generalized stage of the epidemic, with more than 5% of the population affected, has been reached in southern and eastern Africa, together with a few West African countries.

Microeconomic impact

Unlike malaria, HIV/AIDS can affect all strata of society equally. The impact at household level can be measured in terms of the cost of adult deaths, but there are numerous other effects in subsistence economies, including reduction in quality and quantity of farm labor, withdrawal of children from school, and direct financial impact of payment for medical costs and funeral expenses.

Households can be surprisingly resilient because of the coping strategies they often adopt. However, such strategies may include selling assets, contributing to a downward welfare spiral. For example, in Thailand 41% of families with an AIDS death sold land, and 60% of Ugandans sold property to pay for care costs.

Macroeconomic impact

There is no agreement on the true macroeconomic effects of HIV/AIDS. It was originally thought that mortality had little direct effect on the economy in countries where there was an existing high level of unemployment. More recently, it has been argued that there is a strong negative impact on GDP. In addition to losses of labor, survivors are less productive because of the need to care for sick relatives. There is a particularly worrying effect in the education sector: A loss of teachers and the transfer of scarce funds to health services reduce future growth prospects. In Zambia, for example, more teachers die than can be replaced through existing training facilities.

In North Africa, it is estimated that economic growth equivalent to 35% of today's GDP would be forfeited by 2025 compared to a situation where HIV/AIDS was not present. For sub-Saharan Africa, estimates of annual GDP loss per capita in individual countries range from 1.2% for Mozambique to 3.2% for Botswana.

Alleviation of the challenge

For full effectiveness, measures must target both prevention and treatment. However, this analysis looks primarily at prevention, given the rapid changes in drug prices and the lack of clear data on treatment outcome that make calculating the cost-benefit ratio of treatment difficult.

In countries with nascent epidemics, measures would clearly focus on preventive measures among high risk groups. As the epidemic grows within these groups, treatment of sufferers must be added. As a generalized epidemic develops, this package of measures must be implemented on a wider scale. Such interventions may have positive side effects in terms of reduced levels of other sexually transmitted diseases and overall better health education.

Economic evaluation

For North Africa, where the epidemic is still nascent, relatively modest interventions such as increasing condom use by 30% and increasing access to safe needles for intra-venous drug users by 20% could reduce GDP loss by 20% by 2025. However, a delay of even a few years would make this approach considerably less effective.

Figures from Thailand demonstrate the effectiveness of this strategy where disease prevalence in the at-risk groups is high. A policy of 100% condom use in the sex industry is estimated to have averted 200,000 infections between 1993 and 2000, at a cost of Int $1.7 billion. The net benefit is nearly Int $25 billion: a benefit-cost ratio of 14.9.

In SSA, where infection rates are high, a range of indi-vidual interventions all have high benefit-cost ratios. Such measures can also be integrated with delivery of other healthcare programs, for instance, for tuberculosis, to give even greater benefits.

Lastly, a program of integrated measures for low- and middle-income countries was evaluated on the basis that, without intervention, over 45 million new infections would occur between 2002 and 2010. It was estimated that 63% of these cases could be averted, giving a benefit of nearly Int $3 trillion over this period. Total costs were estimated to be Int $59 billion, a benefit-cost ratio of about 50. Sufficient funds would be available if OECD countries donated 0.04% of their Gross National Income.

Strengthening basic health services

Providing a proper infrastructure of primary healthcare has been estimated to address 90% of total medical demands. It has been argued that this is the least costly and most effective way to address global health problems. There is evidence for links between total healthcare expenditure and welfare of particular population groups. More specifically, the World Bank's 1993 World Development Report identified a minimum package of measures. This includes comprehensive immunization, a range of public health programs, and clinical care in pregnancy, for sick children, and in other specific circumstances. Such services would help to meet the health-related Millennium Development Goals, themselves vital if goals in other areas are to be met.

Increasing public spending on health in a group of poor countries from 2% of GDP in 1999 to 15% in 2015 was calculated to cost an additional Int $225 billion. However, it would yield benefits of Int $874 billion to children under five, giving a benefit-cost ratio of nearly 4, with additional benefits for people of other ages, (although the benefit-cost ratio depends crucially on the assumptions made on trends in baseline mortality).

Providing the World Bank-recommended package of interventions to the nearly one billion people in low- and middle-income countries would cost Int $337 billion annually, but would deliver Int $871 billion in benefits, a benefit-cost ratio of 2.6.

This approach may be more difficult to implement than those which are disease-specific. This partly is a reflection of greater international willingness to finance more focused initiatives, and partly the difficulty in effectively delivering improved general health services to the very poor. However, effective treatment over the long term of diseases such as malaria and AIDS requires adequate infrastructure, so there is the opportunity to ensure a wider range of benefits by strengthening basic health services.

Establishing effective health services is not simply a funding task. Aid must be targeted appropriately and spent wisely to deliver the benefits. Some studies, for example, have shown no significant relationship between public spending and child mortality. Such failings are generally policy-related and have their origin in problems such as poor targeting of resources, too little funding reaching local service providers, or too few trained staff. This does not mean the investment should not be made, merely that the difficulties must be appreciated and tackled.

Discussion and conclusions

Estimates suggest that many interventions to improve health care would be highly beneficial to low- and middle-income countries, and evidence from real-world programs shows that benefits are likely to outstrip costs substantially. There are real difficulties – both political and financial – in ensuring successful control of communicable diseases in developing countries. However, the benefits to human welfare are matched by the large economic gains, and we surely should see action in this area as a high priority.

COMMUNICABLE DISEASES

In their challenge paper, Anne Mills and Sam Shillcutt make a compelling case for strong international efforts to tackle the problem of communicable disease. Their opponents have now made further significant contributions to the debate: Jacques van der Gaag argues for some more radical thinking in the area, and David Evans looks more at the detailed reasoning behind the proposals.

Van der Gaag argues that effectively meeting the challenge requires more than putting money into conventional schemes, often based on best-case data from controlled experiments. Putting them into effect on a large scale is often far more difficult and rarely delivers the same benefits. When it comes to delivery methods, donors are often content with the status quo, and governments may lack the political will to take proper action.

In the case of malaria, he fully agrees with the need to tackle the disease and the benefits of doing so. However, although cost effective interventions exist theoretically, in practice delivery mechanisms are woefully inadequate. Despite occasional success stories, as in KwaZulu Natal, the international Roll Back Malaria program has succeeded only in doubling expenditures with little impact on the burden of disease. One reason for this may be the complete reliance on public healthcare infrastructure.

HIV/AIDS is arguably an even greater problem, with 15,000 new cases each week and little progress being made to treat the approximately 40 million existing cases. Recent models predict economic collapse in badly affected countries unless immediate and far-reaching action is taken. Van der Gaag believes that the challenge paper does not go far enough in its proposals: For example, aggressive programs to prevent further infection can be effective (for example, as in Thailand), but the authors make no mention of the need for treatment for those already with the disease.

The problem, he argues, is that governments have generally failed to provide the basic health service infrastructure necessary for the AIDS epidemic to be treated. In sub-Saharan Africa, three-quarters of the people receiving treatment rely on the private sector. However, international donors will not provide funds to the private sector. If donors are willing to give billions of dollars, but governments cannot spend it effectively, surely all other channels, including the private sector, should be considered. This probably means that costs will increase, but currently money is not being spent wisely.

Van der Gaag challenges Mills and Shillcutt's recommendations for increased spending on health service provisions. In his view, there is a very small effect of such spending on health. The more important factors, such as income, education, and access to safe water and sanitation, have been ignored. This means that the benefit-cost ratio for increased public health care spending is actually far lower than stated.

He also makes the point that, in most developing countries, the vast majority of publicly provided healthcare services are consumed by the better-off and do not reach the poor. At the same time, private suppliers are not allowed to compete. The seriousness of the disease burden – much of it avoidable – is such that all alternatives to the current options should be tried. Costs may be higher, but benefits also may be much greater.

Evans, in his opposition paper, takes a more favorable view of the opportunities that form the basis of the challenge paper. However, he casts doubt on some of the figures used in the analysis. In particular, he questions the appropriateness of making comparisons between different interventions, since some are based on the impact of health on GDP (macroeconomic effect) and some on the estimated monetary value of welfare benefits (microeconomic analysis). In many cases, health care programs may do little for economic growth, and may therefore be rejected. Evans believes that analysis based on cost-effectiveness criteria (how much welfare is created for a given input) is more reliable and useful for policy makers.

The Cost Of Illness framework seeks to include all direct costs (treatment, transport, etc.) and indirect costs (loss of earnings, etc). However, this leads to an imperfect assessment of the true burden of disease on households, and is even more misleading when projected in terms of overall GDP loss. Although accurate estimates of monetary costs are difficult to make, the destruction of households and the social fabric caused by disease (AIDS in particular) is all too real. The effects on labor are also substantial: Life expectancy at birth in Southern Africa was 43 years in 2002, but in the absence of AIDS would have been 56.

Evans agrees with van der Gaag that the challenge paper underestimates the costs of AIDS interventions, because it does not take account of treatment costs in countries where the emphasis is on prevention. This would add significantly to the cost. Nevertheless, the benefit-cost ratio is so large that the extra costs would be easily justified.

Evans also makes the same point as van der Gaag about government spending on health: There is little evidence to show that this has a significant impact, whereas money spent on health education has much more effect. Although not proposing the more radical approach advocated in the other opponent paper, he still believes that intense effort is needed to ensure health services can deliver results. One aspect of this is to develop new and better ways for government and non-government sectors to work together and to look at new ways of organizing and delivering services.

There are still large funding gaps to be filled – nearly $4 billion to treat half the total number of HIV/AIDS sufferers by 2005 – even without dealing with the associated problem of TB. There are additional costs associated with providing the basic healthcare infrastructure needed to deliver the potential benefits.

Evans makes one final point about the ethical dimension of using economic analysis to prioritize programs to fight disease. Implicitly, they value human life in poor countries less than in richer countries. On a global scale, this is likely to focus attention on fighting diseases primarily of the developed world, such as cardiovascular disease, rather than scourges such as HIV/AIDS and malaria.

PAUL COLLIER AND ANKE HOEFFLER[1]

3 The Challenge of Reducing the Global Incidence of Civil War

Introduction and overview

Although wars between nations have become less common in recent decades, the frequency of civil wars around the world has increased. These two types of conflict cannot sensibly be analyzed together, so this chapter focuses entirely on reducing the incidence of civil wars.

Three main approaches are discussed:

- Conflict prevention.
- Shortening conflicts.
- Post-conflict policies.

Since the post-conflict period actually presents particularly high risks, the biggest opportunity lies in preventing wars from recurring.

---

[1] Centre for the Study of African Economies, Department of Economics, Oxford University.

The benefits of reducing the incidence of civil war

Benefits from reducing conflict and war accrue at three distinct levels: national, regional and global.

Taking the national level first, one clear cost of civil war is a reduction in economic growth. Using a conservative estimate, one year of conflict reduces a country's growth rate by 2.2%. Since, on average, each civil conflict lasts for seven years, the economy will be 15% smaller at the end of the war than if the war had not taken place. During the post-war recovery, even though the economy on average grows at an annual rate of more than 1% above the norm, it will take roughly 10 years to return to its pre-war growth rates (that is, 17 years after the conflict started). 21 years after the start of the original war, the GDP has returned to the level it would have achieved if no war had occurred. The total economic cost, expressed as a present value at the start of the war (using a 5% discount rate), is 105% of the GDP at that point. This seems to be a fairly conservative estimate, as a more detailed analysis shows the actual figure to lie in the range 41–305% (90% confidence limits).

The welfare of a country's population is further reduced because of increased military spending during and after the war. It is estimated that military spending increases by about 1.8% during the war, and only falls back by 0.5% once the conflict has ended. Assuming that this higher level of spending lasts for only 10 years after the conflict, the additional cost (expressed again as present value when the conflict started) is 18% of GDP.

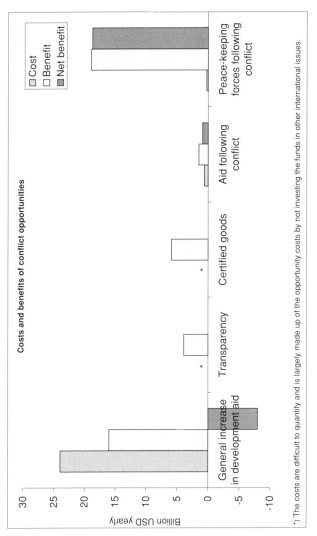

*) The costs are difficult to quantify and is largely made up of the opportunity costs by not investing the funds in other international issues.

Figure 3.1. Cost and benefits of reducing conflicts

41

In addition, conflict has a severe effect on human health. One way of summarizing this effect is to express the cost in terms of Disability Affected Life-Years (DALYs): a measure of the total number of people affected and the period for which their disability lasts. An average war causes an estimated 0.5 million DALYs each year. Assuming they decline smoothly to zero in the 21st year, and discounting them at 5% as for the direct economic costs, gives a figure of 5 million DALYs as the net present value of health costs when hostilities start. If each DALY is valued at $1,000 (roughly the per capita income in many at-risk countries), the economic cost of harm to human health in a typical war is around $5 billion.

At the regional level, analysis shows that the growth rate of neighboring countries not directly involved in the conflict is reduced by 0.9% during the war. If they subsequently recover at the same rate as the conflict country, the additional cost (as a present value at the start of the conflict) is 43% of initial GDP. On average, each country has 2.7 neighbors, so the direct effect of a typical civil war on neighboring countries is 115% of the initial GDP of one country: greater than the direct effect in the conflict country itself.

There is also an effect on military spending in adjoining countries: a neighborhood arms race often ensues. In the average case considered so far, a 1% rise in military expenditure in the country at war would increase the average spending of bordering countries by 0.23%. In a typical conflict, that means military spending will increase by 0.4% of GDP during the war, and by 0.3% during the post-conflict period: a total net present value of 4.3% of the country's initial

GDP. On average, there are 2.7 neighboring countries; thus the total extra cost of the regional arms race is about 12% of one country's GDP.

Other costs which are too difficult to quantify are incurred both in the country at war and in the region as a whole, including forced migration. With the proviso that the figures so far are therefore underestimated to some degree, the total benefit of averting a single "typical" civil war can be calculated. The various national and regional costs covered so far amount to 250% of initial GDP. The average GDP of conflict-affected low-income countries (excluding India and China) just prior to war is $19.7 billion. Therefore, the cost of a single war is around $49 billion. To this we must add $5 billion of health costs, giving a total cost of $54 billion for a single low-income country.

This is already a significant figure, but in addition there is the "conflict trap": Countries that have just experienced a civil war are more likely to have further conflict. Looking at the 21 countries in which wars started and ended in the period 1965–99, the risk of conflict over the five years before the war averaged 22.3%, but this rose to 38.6% post-war. Over the 15-year period needed for the risk to reach the pre-war level again, the additional discounted cost is $10.2 billion. Thus the total national and regional cost of a single war is more than $64 billion.

There are additional, global impacts of civil wars, massive in scale but difficult to assign a cost to. Three world scourges over the last 30 years have had civil conflicts as contributory factors: hard drug production, AIDS, and international terrorism.

Based on these estimates (and bearing in mind the unquantified but significant global effects of conflict), we can look at the benefits of reducing the number of countries at war at any one time. At present, an average of two civil wars start each year. The net cost of these would be $128 billion. So, an initiative which reduced the chance of a new war by 10%, for example, would generate benefits of around $13 billion each year.

Another class of opportunities are those which shorten wars rather than prevent them. The benefit of shortening the typical war by one year – from seven to six years – turns out to be surprisingly large: nearly $11 billion. For the average of two new conflicts per year, this would generate benefits of about $22 billion annually. There would also be a one-off gain from shortening the present 17 significant civil conflicts by one year. A discounted value of this figure (comparable to the year-on-year benefit) is around $9 billion, so the total annual benefit of shortening civil wars by one year is over $30 billion.

Opportunities for conflict prevention

Analysis shows that a country's political and social characteristics are much less important than economic factors in determining the risk of war. The three most significant characteristics are level of income, its rate of income growth, and the degree of dependence upon primary commodity exports.

Of the two wars that on average start annually, 0.7 occur in the poor, relatively small countries with no recent history of war (China and India are excluded because or their sheer size). Here we look at the benefits of preventing some of these. Post-conflict situations represent a separate opportunity.

Raising the economic growth rate reduces the risk of conflict both directly and by increasing incomes. As a point of reference, a 1% increase in annual growth rate for a period of 10 years was modeled. For the first five years, the model shows a reduction in the risk of war from 13.8% to 12.7% as the average risk of a war breaking out in a poor country with no recent war. During the second five-year period, the additional income level effect reduces the risk further, to 12.2%. Assuming that the growth rate returns to normal after the 10 year period, the longer term effect of higher income leaves the risk of conflict at 12.7%, as a permanent reduction over the initial level.

In financial terms, the benefit in the first five years is an 8% reduction in the chance of a civil war starting. Since each war costs $64 billion, and on average 0.7 start each year, the annual benefit is $3.6 billion. In the second five-year period, this gain rises to $5.4 billion annually (a 12% reduction in the risk of conflict starting). After 10 years, the annual benefit falls back to $3.6 billion. The present value (discounted at 5%) is around $79 billion. To put this large figure in perspective, remember that this is purely a benefit of conflict reduction, over and above the direct benefits of poverty reduction.

Two major policy options might deliver these benefits: aid and better utilization of income from natural resources.

Aid

The effect of aid will depend to a large extent on the political and institutional situation. Additional aid as a means to boost growth is also subject to the law of diminishing returns. On average, for a single country from the group of 32 poor, relatively small, and generally peaceful states, an extra 2% in aid would raise their annual growth rates by only 0.2%. The benefits of aid in terms of conflict reduction would therefore be one-fifth of that from the model of 1% additional GDP growth: $16 billion.

At purchasing power parity rates, the combined GDPs of the countries in this group amount to $1,200 billion, so the overall cost of the additional aid amounts to $24 billion annually. The net present value of this over a decade is $195 billion. This indicates that unselective aid programs are not a cost effective way of reducing conflict: The benefits are less than 10% of the costs. This is not to say that the aid may not be justified; after all, its main purpose is poverty reduction. However, conflict reduction should not be expected to be a major outcome.

Improved governance of income from natural resources

Not only is income from natural resources poorly converted to growth in many conflict-prone countries, but revenue from primary commodities is actually a risk factor in civil war. There are a number of reasons for this, including the fact that valuable resources can encourage regional secessions and provide finance for rebel movements.

There are two ways in which the international community can act collectively to improve this situation:

1. Increase the transparency of revenue streams. A particular campaign, backed by a range of NGOs, the G8 governments, and international institutions is known as the Extractive Industries Transparency Initiative (EITI).
2. Encourage greater medium-term revenue smoothing to avoid destabilizing booms and busts.

Such international action would provide a template for government reform and would give clear guidelines against which poorly performing governments could be measured. International agreements are difficult to achieve, and only a limited number can be negotiated at one time. There is therefore an opportunity cost of pursuing this particular strategy in preference to some other initiative that could also bring equal or greater benefits.

It should be feasible to halve the adverse effects of poorly managed natural resource incomes (complete elimination may be an overly ambitious target). This would create a knock-on effect: reducing conflicts via increased growth rates. To halve the adverse effects, growth rates would be raised by 0.067%, assumed to be permanent once reforms are in place. The benefit in present value terms would be $12.1 billion.

There is also a much larger benefit realizable. Greater transparency in the revenue flows can reduce regional grievances and the incentives for secessionist groups to take control of the income. If such action reduced the risk from natural resource dependence by 10%, the overall risk of war for a typical country would fall from 13.8% to 12.7%. This would be worth $3.9 billion annually and, assuming it is permanent, gives a present value benefit of $77 billion.

The total benefit from conflict reduction by this route is then $89 billion.

Opportunities for shortening conflicts

Civil wars last typically for seven years. Unfortunately, there is no systematic evidence of the effectiveness of either financial or military intervention by the international community. However, rebel movements tend to be self-financing, so controlling international markets in commodities and armaments could reduce their ability to be self-sustaining.

When the world was alerted to the problem of "conflict diamonds" as a funding source for rebel movements in Africa, a government certification process was put in place. This appears to have been at least partly responsible for the collapse of both the RUF in Sierra Leone and UNITA in Angola, and the concept is now being extended to trade in timber. Certification does not totally exclude rebel groups from the market, but it introduces a two-tier market where uncertified goods are sold at a discount.

In addition to diamonds and timber (and extending this to oil), it is even conceivable to consider creating a two-tier market in hard drugs, 95% of which originate from civil war environments. This would be analogous to the situation in the UK in the 1960s, where registered addicts could obtain drugs legitimately via the country's health service.

In 2002, conflict diamonds were trading at an approximately 10% discount. This figure can be taken as a minimum expectation, since diamonds are difficult to police and proper monitoring was not in place at the time. Using a 10% discount as an estimate for commodities in general, and using a figure of 12% for the conflict shortening effect (derived from estimates of the actual effect of commodity price changes), this would reduce the length of the war by a little under a year. Given the number of countries which significantly depend upon commodity exports, we arrive at a figure of $5.9 billion for the present value of this intervention.

Reducing post-conflict risks

During the first decade following a war, there are very high risks of repeat conflict: around half of all civil wars arise in this way. However, typically there are only about 12 countries in this post-conflict category at any given time, making it relatively easy to direct resources to them. Two policy approaches to reduce post-conflict risks are the use of aid, and military spending.

Post-conflict aid

Countries typically have higher growth rates in the post-conflict decade, but these are neither assured nor evenly spread. Growth is, in fact, driven entirely by the amount of aid, and is concentrated in the middle years of the decade. Although the need is great immediately post-conflict, there is limited capacity to use aid effectively; by the middle years, resources can be managed better and the needs addressed properly. The opportunity identified is then to provide increased aid at the time when it is most useful: The analysis is for an aid increase of 2% of GDP for the middle five years of the decade.

There are typically 12 countries in their first post-conflict decade at any one time, with a combined GDP of about $163 billion. The cost of the additional aid averages $1.6 billion per year over the decade, with a net present value of $13 billion. The gain in growth rate in the years when extra aid is received would be 1.1%, more than five times the increase seen in normal non-conflict situations. The benefits of this targeted aid in terms of avoiding conflict can be calculated as $31.5 billion across the 12 countries. This intervention is clearly cost-effective for the additional security benefits alone, in addition to its main purpose of poverty reduction.

Military expenditure

In a country's vulnerable years immediately post-war, government military spending is maintained at a high level and actually appears to be counter-productive in terms of peace-keeping. There is a case for international military intervention, on condition that the government makes deep cuts in its own military expenditure. Merely by reducing this spending to pre-conflict levels, GDP would increase by 2% in the decade.

Assuming that an international peace-keeping force completely avoids the outbreak of another war during the ten years it is in place, a risk of 38.6% in the first five years and 31.9% in the second is averted. With the average civil war costing $64 billion, the present value of this intervention is $29.9 billion. In addition, a gain of $3.2 billion can be attributed to the reduced risk of war because of reduced military spending and increased GDP, making a total of $33.1 billion.

Costs will vary with the individual country's situation, but as a typical example the current British force in Sierra Leone has cost, on average, $49 million each year. If we assume that such forces will be in place for the full 10 years, the net present value comes to only $397 million. The benefit-cost ratio is therefore enormous: an expenditure of less than half a billion dollars securing a benefit of $30 billion. Extending this approach to all 12 typical post-conflict situations would deliver a benefit of $397 billion for a cost of less than $5 billion.

Conclusion and comparison

All the estimates in this chapter are gross approximations. Nevertheless, they enable us to distinguish between those policies offering very high rates of return and those which are uneconomic. Clearly, the option of international military intervention under Chapter VII of the United Nations Charter offers enormous benefits, but is also the most difficult politically. At the other end of the scale, aid has very limited effectiveness in conflict prevention unless it is much better targeted. Reforms of the commodity trading system fall between the extremes, offering significant benefits at reasonable cost.

THE CHALLENGE OF CONFLICTS
OPPONENTS' VIEWS

In their challenge paper, Paul Collier and Anke Hoeffler estimate the costs of civil war and propose a number of opportunities to reduce their total incidence. Their favored options in economic terms are to avoid conflicts recurring by targeted use of aid or international military intervention. Tony Addison and Michael Intriligator make constructive criticisms of the analysis and conclusions in their separate opponent papers.

While acknowledging that the challenge paper presents the most comprehensive estimate to date of the cost of a typical war, Addison has some concerns about the authors' methodology. In particular, he criticizes their valuation of Disability Adjusted Life Years (DALYs), necessary to calculate the health costs of conflict. Collier and Hoeffler use a figure of $1,000, effectively valuing the economic loss rather than the value of life itself. He regards this approach as largely discredited, and supports instead a "willingness-to-pay" valuation of life, which typically gives figures some five times greater.

Addison's second criticism of methodology relates to the discount rate used (5%). This is a mechanism to account for a preference to receive a benefit now rather than a larger one at some time in the future. He believes there is a case for DALYs not to be discounted at all, but accepts that, whatever the methodology used, a constant discount rate must be used for opportunities across all challenges to allow them to be ranked properly.

Moving to the opportunities themselves, Addison's view is that the value of aid in conflict prevention has been understated because, properly targeted, it can have far-reaching effects. However, he also recognizes that poorly targeted aid can actually do great harm to the prospects for peace when it merely bolsters dictatorships and allows inequality to grow.

He agrees that the proposal for the improvement of transparency in handling natural resources is sound, since billions of dollars of revenue are diverted from the public purse, but thinks the potential benefits are overstated. Nevertheless, since costs are low, the net benefit of implementation would still be large.

Collier and Hoeffler's second identified opportunity is to shorten conflicts by reducing rebel access to commodity markets, as has already been done successfully for "conflict diamonds" via the Kimberley process. Addison suggests that conflicts could similarly be shortened by means of agricultural trade liberalization. For example, removing subsidies to American cotton farmers would raise the international value of the crop relative to opium, giving growers in conflict countries such as Afghanistan the option of an alternative livelihood.

When it comes to reducing post-conflict risks by delaying aid until the state is in a position to use the money properly, Addison takes issue with the authors of the challenge paper. In his view, aid is needed immediately post-conflict both for poverty reduction and to ensure that sound institutions are put in place. He also questions the estimate for the cost of foreign peace-keeping troops, which he thinks could be much higher in some cases (indeed, in Afghanistan it runs at about $1 billion a month). Nevertheless, he thinks that this is a valuable suggestion, particularly if developing country troops can be used.

Finally, Addison makes his own additional proposal: to reduce the intensity of conflicts, (as measured by the number of casualties). This would include, for example, measures to reduce the flow of weapons, to bring war crimes suspects to justice, and to protect refugees.

Intriligator takes a somewhat different, and broader, perspective. In his view, Collier and Hoeffler's conclusion that the highest payoff would come from interventions to prevent conflicts restarting in post-war situations is questionable. In particular, he draws attention to the huge costs of wars in their early stages – Rwanda being a recent case in point – and believes that public policy should focus on a balanced approach to all three opportunities.

Moving to the first of the three opportunities – conflict prevention – Intriligator is doubtful that higher growth fueled by international aid will necessarily lead to a lower incidence of civil war. Equally, he points to examples of countries heavily dependent on exports from extractive industries that have not had a civil war, so doubts that greater transparency in this area is necessary or effective in all cases. Instead, he emphasizes the need to reduce access to arms and other resources for the potentially warring parties (for example, the Oscar Arias proposal for an embargo on all arms shipments to sub-Saharan Africa), and to use peacekeeping forces and the tools of diplomacy to prevent conflicts.

He believes that there are other ways to reduce the length of conflicts (the second opportunity) including economic sanctions and the use of small, well-targeted UN peacekeeping missions (which have been more successful than larger ones).

His doubts about the use of aid extend also to its proposed use to reduce the chance of conflict restarting (the third opportunity). Equally, he thinks the focus on the use of international military intervention only for this opportunity is too narrow. Selective use of all the tools can be beneficial in preventing conflicts occurring in the first place, reducing their intensity, and avoiding them flaring up again.

While there are clearly major challenges presented by civil wars, Intriligator also believes that the dangers of international wars should receive more consideration. Indeed, such factors as regional conflicts developing into wider problems, regional arms races, international arms sales, and proliferation of nuclear weapons present major challenges, which might be addressed in part in the same ways as proposed for civil wars.

In summary, the two opponents agree wholeheartedly that reducing the incidence of civil conflict is a global challenge that demands our attention, but have different views on the most effective way of doing this.

4 Toward a New Consensus for Addressing the Global Challenge of the Lack of Education

The scope of the challenge and a framework

"Lack of education" as a global challenge must be understood, at an individual level, as a failure to master the many distinct competencies necessary to thrive in a modern economy and society. Remedying this is not simply a question of providing more schools, more teaching aids, or reducing drop-out rates. The challenge is to create competencies and learning achievement rather than just educational tools.

Because it is easy to measure, data on enrolment (the percentage of school-age children actually starting school) is often used as a proxy for educational progress. However, enrolment levels have little bearing on actual achievement. For example, a large part of the educational deficit results from drop-outs rather than failure to enrol. Likewise, substantial gaps in attainment between students from richer and poorer households occur in all countries.

Most importantly – and disappointingly – levels of learning achievement in nearly all developing countries are abysmally low. Only former Soviet bloc countries and the Southeast Asian tiger economies achieve results comparable to those of OECD members. In recent tests, virtually all developing countries perform far worse than Greece (the poorest performing major OECD country). Only 3.1% of Indonesian students scored higher in reading competency than the *average* French student, and the average Brazilian maths student achieves the same as the bottom 2% of Danes.

Poor performance is caused, at least in part, by systems that are geared to measure inputs (money spent, schools constructed, etc.) instead of students' performance. Also, in many countries, the entire system is seriously deficient, with school infrastructure being inadequate, the most basic teaching materials (pencils, paper, chalk, textbooks) in short supply, and teachers poorly trained, supervised, and monitored. In lower- and middle-income countries, there is a severe lack of educational achievement, but it is not due to children not enrolling in school.

In summary, this challenge requires several factors to be addressed so that mastery of basic competencies can be achieved:

- Increasing the competence of children entering school.
- Increasing learning achievement at school by –
  - Reducing the number of children who never enrol
  - Reducing late enrolment
  - Increasing the number of years schooling completed by each student.
- Increasing the competence gain per year of schooling.

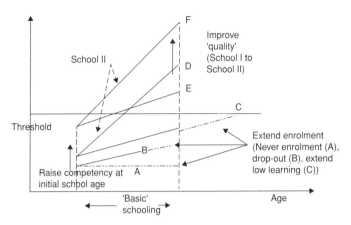

Figure 4.1. How to raise the levels of competence through schooling: the proximate determinants of learning achievement

Analytical framework for evaluating opportunities

None of these proximate factors is directly under the direct control of national or regional policy makers: outcomes are determined by individual decisions of children, parents, and teachers. Many opportunities can be proposed, but to be credible there must be a coherent causal chain from proposed action to desired output; it is not good enough to state that simply building more schools will mean higher enrolment.

Demand

Parents and children make decisions about schooling by balancing expected benefits (for instance, increased income or better health) against costs (for instance, books, uniform, and travel, plus the opportunity cost of the child doing something else). Even if the benefits exceed the costs, demand may be constrained by lack of current income.

Supply

Formal schooling can in principle be supplied by either the public or private sectors (including commercial companies, religious organizations, and NGOs). Supply is virtually unconstrained in the longer term, although schooling provided at below market cost clearly *is* limited.

What opportunities exist and how can they be assessed?

Improvements to educational achievement may arise either through policy action or systemic reform. Below, four policy options are considered:

- Expanding provision by building or expanding schools (supply-side).
- Improving quality with targeted increases in expenditures (supply-side).
- Direct support to households to reduce the real costs of schooling (demand-side).
- Raising the benefits of schooling (demand-side).

But policy changes may not be enough: The present public sector framework may provide the wrong incentives to improve overall standards of basic education. This does not mean that governments cannot provide good quality education – they do indeed provide it in high-performing countries such as Korea or Hungary. This chapter considers systemic reform of the role of government in setting policy, focusing on outcomes, incentives, and responsibilities.

Evaluating the four opportunities for policy action

In this section, the various policy options are assessed for their potential to produce high returns in tackling the challenge of poor educational achievement.

Opportunity 1: Supply side; expanding the quantity of schools

A commitment to universal primary education has been a high priority in development programs for many years. However, it is generally assumed that providing more money for governments to build schools will effectively increase take-up of education. The cost of educating the 100–120 million children who have not yet received primary education has been estimated as between $9.1 billion and $27.6 billion, depending on the assumptions used.

However, these figures might better be interpreted as the cost of providing educational facilities *if* all these children decided to attend. Empirical evidence strongly suggests that provision of spaces is not in itself the answer. Research in small communities in 21 different developing countries showed that, although school construction positively affects enrolment, the impact is very small. For the communities surveyed, enrolment of 6–14 year olds averaged 53.2%. Building a primary school in every community would only marginally increase this, to 55.4%.

Similarly, analysis of the District Primary Education Project (DPEP) in India shows that the $1.62 billion spent since 1994 to expand and improve the quality of schooling has increased enrolment by only 1–2% compared with areas not in the program.

While in some remote areas supply is a key constraint, simply expanding the school system is not the general answer.

Opportunity 2: Improving quality; supply side policy actions

Raising the quality of education would have multiple positive impacts, including reducing the drop-out rate, increasing overall enrolment, and raising the level of achievement of those already enrolled. The question that looms is whether increased spending per pupil is sufficient, or serious systemic reform is necessary to realize the benefits of additional expenditure.

In simple terms, certain combinations of teaching services and instructional materials lead to particular learning achievements. Assuming that the balance between teaching and materials is not optimized, a given expenditure will have much better results if it is spent on the input that is furthest from optimum. For example, there would be little point in employing more teachers if learning was constrained by a severe shortage of textbooks or writing materials.

This framework can be used, for example, to analyze the evidence on class size, which illustrates four fundamental points:

1. Smaller class size is only good for education in some cases. If learning is already effective, a smaller class will

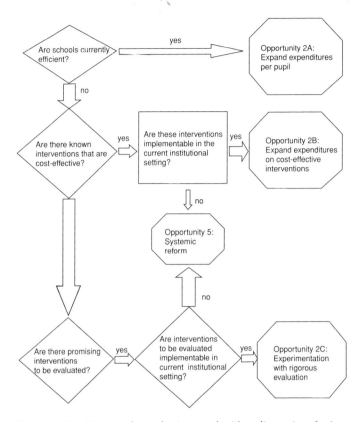

Figure 4.2. Decision tree for evaluating supply-side policy actions for improving education

have no effect, but reducing the size of a very large class may be a significant positive factor.

2. There seems to be a small (less than 3%) increase in student scores in some subjects when class sizes are reduced by five from a typical level of 25 students. For poorer countries, where class sizes may be much larger,

there can be real and significant effects (supported by evidence from apartheid-era South Africa and Bolivia).

3. Only a fraction of the variation in learning achievement can be attributed to differences between schools. Much of the difference in achievement occurs within schools, and a large part of the remainder is due to differences in student background. Typically, a maximum of about 20% of student performance can be attributed to school performance.

4. Class sizes as determined by public policy do not necessarily represent the optimum use of resources. Although smaller class sizes in some circumstances may be very beneficial, in other cases there may be no positive effect (for instance, if poorly trained teachers are unable to apply appropriate teaching methods).

2A: Overall budget expansion Increased funding of education alone rarely achieves increased quality, and crude proxies such as class size or share of GDP say nothing about achievement. Indeed, during 1970–1994, OECD countries significantly increased real expenditures per pupil, but estimated learning achievement in maths and science at best made very modest gains – and in most cases actually decreased.

The current consensus amongst education specialists is that extra spending on education in developing countries is necessary, but will only increase quality if

a) The extra budget is targeted at highly productive activities (Opportunity 2B).

b) It is devoted to, or combined with, new educational techniques (Opportunity 2C).

c) It is accompanied by systemic reform.

2B: Targeted expansion of particular elements of the education system. Improved attainment levels could be aided by interventions in three categories: instructional materials, key infrastructure, and teacher training. Such interventions would almost certainly have substantial, cost-effective impacts on learning achievement. The particular interventions will depend on the individual circumstances of the countries, regions, and schools.

However, cause and effect are difficult to determine, given the large influence of parental choice and the fact that additional educational inputs may be ineffective if the school itself is dysfunctional.

Effective changes are not easy to implement. There are many examples of teacher training initiatives that have had no positive impact on educational achievement. Moreover, if a particular change would dramatically improve attainment levels, why has it not already occurred? The conclusion is that the present policy system does not offer appropriate incentives to improve efficiency.

2C: Experimentation with rigorous evaluation. Rigorous evaluations of the impact of interventions are carried out infrequently. They often produce surprising results that challenge the conventional wisdom about the effectiveness of particular actions.

Impact evaluations of interventions should be carried out more readily: not just "before and after" studies, but also "with and without" as a better measure of the true effect. However, the results must also be used as a basis for future improvements: If they are ignored, they have zero value.

To summarize, supply-side improvements to quality are clearly possible in a variety of circumstances. However, the present author believes that nearly all developing countries will meet the educational challenge far more effectively via a process of systemic reform.

Opportunity 3: Demand side; raising the benefits of schooling

There are two demand-side opportunities that are indirect, but may be strongly correlated with educational achievement. Moreover, these are not education specific: Their general positive impact will probably make them cost-effective even without considering effects on education.

3A: The effect of income on education. Household factors – income and parental education – are strongly correlated with educational outcome. International comparisons suggest that a child from a rich household where both parents have had five years schooling would be 28% more likely to be enrolled at school than a poor child with uneducated parents. Over time, such factors can have large social effects, such as in Vietnam, where significant reductions in child labor (with presumably large increases in school enrolment) occurred as households emerged from poverty. Because such demand-side changes occur relatively slowly, so does the transition from moderate to near universal uptake of basic education.

3B: The effect of raising returns to education. In situations where the apparent benefits are low (i.e., stagnant economic and technological conditions), parents may decide not to send their children to school, or may discourage their children from staying in school. However, evidence suggests that parents respond positively to perceived increased returns, and the catalyst is often technological change. For instance, the "green revolution" of the 1970s introduced high-yielding, dwarf varieties of rice and wheat, and increased farm profits significantly. Regions of India that adopted the new technology experienced a large increases in the return on education and these resulted in significant expansions of education.

Opportunity 4: Demand side; direct support that lowers the cost of schooling

Various initiatives can reduce the household cost of education. On an economic basis, these should clearly increase the demand for schooling.

Blanket fee reductions can increase school enrolment. Experience in Africa with fee elimination shows that initial enrolment increases dramatically, but it does not necessarily translate to higher attainment at secondary school level. Reductions in school budgets because of lost income may indeed *reduce* overall quality.

Other interventions, such as targeted programs (provision of school meals, for example) or conditional cash transfers, can also have a significant impact on enrolment. The cost-effectiveness of such measures depends on the details, but cash transfers are primarily a poverty-reduction tool, and making them conditional upon school enrolment carries no additional cost.

The fifth element: Systemic reform to create performance management and producer accountability

In its 2004 World Development Report, the World Bank argued that public provision of schooling has in-built, systemic failures to deliver quality education. It believes that institutional conditions create a lack of incentives to produce performance-oriented management.

In non-authoritarian societies, accountability is achieved by citizens expressing their demands via the political system, thus sending clear signals to the public sector suppliers. An equally viable proposition is for resources to be transferred directly to citizens to allow them their own choice of schooling (within an appropriate regulatory framework). This is not to suggest that public provision of education cannot work well: Some of the world's best educational systems are public.

No simple overall system provides universal high quality education. Reasonably effective systems differ widely, from extreme decentralization in the USA to tight centralization in France. Also, both Singapore and Nigeria have schooling systems based on the English model, but with diametrically opposed outcomes. There are also a number of credible alternative approaches to direct public provision.

Whatever the system, it must address four challenges at once:

- *Clear objectives* must be established, and performance must be measured against them. Schools are not machines for teaching facts: they are the mechanism whereby societies replicate themselves.
- *Sustained adequate financing*.
- *Autonomy to manage for results*: Accountability for performance means that schools must have the freedom to act independently.
- *Accountability* must be assured via a centralized (for comparability) system of measuring and publicizing school performance.

Combining opportunities in an international program; Education for All/Fast Track Initiative (EFA/FTI)

This initiative is the cutting edge approach to tackling the challenge of lack of education. Donors will provide increasing amounts of aid to countries that provide "credible" plans for meeting the EFA targets. In particular, it encourages more efficient expenditures. Analysis of spending in countries that have successfully attained primary educational goals is used to generate indicative ratios for teacher wages/GDP and class size. If a country has high unit costs for education, the extra cost to meet Millennium Development Goals would not be funded without at least some attempt to reduce the unit cost. The FTI also expects countries to use a coherent, integrated approach, which should incorporate the various opportunities described in this chapter.

THE CHALLENGE OF LACK OF EDUCATION
OPPONENTS' VIEWS

Two quite different views of Lant Pritchett's challenge paper have been put forward. One – by Paul Schultz – is very critical, whereas the other – by Ludger Wößmann – is broadly supportive.

In Schultz's view, Pritchett advances no concrete evidence in support of his view that systemic reform of the education system is the essential way forward. The proposals are entirely hypothetical, and take no account of the powerful entrenched interests that would take considerable political and economic resources to overcome. Without some estimates of these costs and the benefits that would accrue, it is not possible to decide whether this is truly a high worthwhile opportunity.

Schultz also objects to Pritchett giving his main consideration to the most efficient (that is, least costly) delivery of education of a given standard. He believes that the private and social returns on education and the effects of public subsidies are equally important and should have been included in the challenge paper. The prevailing view among international agencies has been that education is a social investment, with returns highest at the primary level.

This is the view that Pritchett has also adopted, concentrating on cost-effective provision of primary education to maximize social returns and reduce inequality of earnings within a society.

However, Shultz refers to more recent evidence that the individual benefits of education are often greater at more advanced levels. So, a public education system designed to reduce inequalities, by focusing on primary schooling, may not be the most effective for individuals or the economy. This conflict between the goals of social equality and economic efficiency has to be resolved before it is possible to decide what truly are the best opportunities for improving education.

In the challenge paper, Pritchett, although cautious, suggests that measures to reduce the private costs of schooling may be productive. However, Schultz is more sceptical, finding little empirical evidence for the successful targeting of incentives to those families who would not otherwise send their children to school. Without such targeting, money would be wasted by unnecessarily subsidizing many other families. Nonetheless, he sees that such an approach could be made to work.

Shultz is yet more sceptical about the vague systematic reforms proposed by Pritchett. He supports the concept of school accountability, but does not see how such basic reforms can be accomplished without broader political reform. Even decentralization of education may not always be the answer, if community schools are effectively run by local elites for their own benefit.

Since basic structural reform is extremely difficult, Shultz argues for more consideration of second-best partial reforms (for example, use of school vouchers to encourage competition between public and private schools). He believes that such small-scale changes could be more effective than the proposed radical reform of the system.

Finally, Schultz raises a very difficult issue for the Copenhagen Consensus. The economic benefits of primary education seem to be declining in parts of the developing world (particularly Africa): Do we therefore conclude that there are already sufficient primary educated workers to meet current economic demands? If so, is the Millennium Development Goal for basic education still justified, if only as a way of reducing inequality?

The second opponent paper takes a far less critical stance. In particular, Wößmann supports the view that institutional reform is clearly needed, in addition to specific resource reforms. However, he feels that there should have been greater justification of some opportunities via cost-benefit analysis.

In contrast to Schultz, Wößmann believes that Pritchett has been too cautious in his assessment of the opportunity to increase demand for schooling by reducing the cost to households. In particular, he makes the case for waiving primary school fees. Pritchett's view is that eliminating school fees may cause a substantial drop in revenue, which would need to be replaced from public funds. Wößmann argues that this is more than offset by the benefits that accrue from better educational attainment. Nevertheless, the funding must be made available some time before the benefits are received.

Data from Uganda shows that, from 1996 to 2001, waiving of fees increased numbers in primary education from 3.4 million to 6.9 million, at an estimated cost of $90 million per year. To set against this, someone with an extra year of schooling receives on average an extra $64 in additional income each year. Applying this to all of the extra 3.5 million children brought into primary schools by waiving fees gives an estimated $3.3 billion in benefits to the Ugandan economy over their working life. This represents a benefit-cost ratio of 37, which suggests that such an option would be highly cost effective even in less favorable circumstances.

On the question of systemic reform, (which Wößmann agrees with in principle), the difficulty lies in defining concrete actions, given the complex nature of the opportunity. He reports that data from international school achievement tests shows better performance in schools that have autonomy in decision making. However, this improved performance is facilitated by use of centralized standard setting and testing to encourage competition and comparisons between schools.

Wößmann agrees with Schultz that the main cost of systemic reform is political, but takes the view that such costs are probably a prerequisite for introducing effective reforms to meet any of the challenges. He considers it a weakness of the original challenge paper that Pritchett chose not to estimate the benefits of broad reform. By his own reckoning, these could lie in the range of 3% (for use of externally set exit exams) to 16% (for the greater effects of school autonomy) of the lifetime earnings for all students. This he considers to be an "astoundingly large" benefit, likely to justify costly reforms.

SUSAN ROSE-ACKERMAN[1]

5 The Challenge of Poor Governance and Corruption

Introduction

Researchers at the World Bank estimate that $1 trillion is spent on bribes annually, some 3% of global GDP. The impact on economic growth and world income could well be much higher than this. Corruption is one symptom of a failure to achieve an appropriate balance between private wealth and public power. Ultimately, there is a risk that government will be captured by powerful interests and rendered dysfunctional. Both private citizens and companies are then drawn into the cycle of bribery, forced to pay corrupt officials to obtain routine services and major contracts and concessions.

Global solutions to this challenge are difficult to find because corruption and poor governance have a variety of causes. Solutions are not easy to implement because they disadvantage powerful vested interests that can block

[1] Henry R Luce Professor of Law and Political Science, Yale University.

reforms. Despite these caveats, carefully tailored policies – carried out with the personal commitment of those on the ground – can have large benefits and very low costs.

Research on the causes and consequences of corruption

Before looking at reform proposals, we should examine the empirical evidence on the causes and consequences of corruption.

Cross-country comparisons show that, on average, rich countries have less reported corruption and better functioning governments than poorer ones. High levels of corruption are associated with lower levels of human development (for example, as measured by the United Nations Human Development Index, a composite measure of health, education, and income). It is tempting, therefore, to think that it may be sufficient to stimulate growth through appropriate economic policies, with good governance being a natural but secondary consequence. However, poor governance is itself a *cause* of poor economic growth, and so more specific reforms are needed to tackle it.

There are two main indices of corruption published by Transparency International (TI, an international advocacy group) and the World Bank. The indices, which are based on similar underlying data, provide a good indication of the relative difficulty of doing business in different countries (although neither index gives a quantitative measure of the amount of corruption in monetary terms).

Analysis of the data from these two organizations shows that high levels of corruption are associated with lower levels of investment and growth. For example, if relatively clean and rich Singapore had the same levels of corruption as relatively corrupt and poor Mexico, the effect on its citizens would be equivalent to a tax increase of more than 20%. Similarly, an increase in a country's TI corruption score by one point is associated with an increase in productivity of 4% of GDP and increases net capital inflows of 0.5% of GDP. This implies that if a country such as Tanzania could achieve the corruption score of the United Kingdom, its GDP would be more than 20% higher and net annual per capita capital inflows would increase by 3%.

As governments spend more on unnecessary and wasteful public infrastructure at the expense of education, health, and the environment, public welfare also suffers. Ignoring the very poorest countries, higher levels of corruption are associated with greater inequality. Government legitimacy is also reduced, which encourages citizens to avoid paying taxes. This in turn reduces the overall size of corrupt governments, making fewer resources available for potentially beneficial projects: a true downward spiral.

At the level of the individual firm, surveys show that corruption has a negative impact on sales and investment growth, and is associated with other factors such as high taxes and financing difficulties. Similar considerations apply to export levels and foreign investment. As an example, it has been suggested that if government effectiveness in Calcutta could be increased so that the city had the same investment climate as Shanghai, exports from private industry could rise from 24% to 47% of output.

Ineffective government breeds corruption. In the ex-Communist states of Central and Eastern Europe, particularly in Russia and Ukraine, there is widespread hiding of sales and salaries from the government, and some firms exist completely "off-the-books." This is a consequence of the corruption of government officials. Household surveys in the region show that most people disapprove of corruption, although they are often party to it (bribes to hospital doctors, traffic police, and customs officials are the most common). More effective government with reduced incentives for bribery would be popular with most people.

Although poor governance, weak economic conditions, and inequality all contribute to corruption, cross-country differences also depend on historical and social factors. Studies have shown, for example, that institutions are generally weaker and corruption greater in countries which are very ethnically fragmented, have few Protestants, and have socialist or French legal origins. Fortunately, such factors become insignificant when income is considered: richer countries have less corruption whatever their historical legacies. High levels of economic freedom lead to greater prosperity and are also correlated with low corruption levels.

Much corruption occurs in the administration of public programs as when bribery is used to evade regulations and taxes. However, the World Bank also identifies what it calls "crony capitalism" or "state capture," where the government effectively serves the interests of a small group of business people and politicians, with or without an element of organized crime. This seems to be a particular problem in former Soviet Union countries. Those firms associated with crony networks thrive, but at the expense of the overall economic health of the nation.

Reform proposals

Policies that just focus on economic growth will not be sufficient to reduce corruption, and such policies will not even produce the desired results unless the state is reasonably well governed. Proposals should therefore address governance issues in a coordinated way. They must also overcome the inevitable resistance from powerful vested interests, which will occur however beneficial the reforms may be to the general population.

Compared to some of the other global challenges – hunger, disease and conflict, for example – corruption does not seem such a pressing issue. However, the weak governance typically associated with corruption also reduces the effectiveness of policy initiatives to tackle them. Improved governance designed to reduce corruption and improve state functioning would make initiatives to tackle other social ills more likely to succeed.

Benefit-cost analysis of reform proposals is difficult although cross-country analysis indicates that the benefits of reducing corruption are large. It is difficult to demonstrate clear effects from individual policies. Nevertheless, some reforms are essentially costless and their benefit-cost ratios therefore are very large.

Although some states may be so dysfunctional that effective reform is not feasible at present, in many cases a concerted application of the following opportunities could have significant benefits. Note that these are not isolated choices; effective reform will require an appropriate mix of these complementary initiatives.

Opportunity 1: Oversight and transparency

Low levels of accountability are associated with low per capita income and a high degree of "crony bias." A specific proposal to correct this is the encouragement of local citizen involvement. The key to its success is to identify wasteful government programs that are suitable for managed decentralization (although data coordination and anti-corruption laws would still be administered centrally). Citizens can be involved either as monitors or as producers and sometimes as both.

There is good empirical evidence of the benefits of improving integrity and increasing transparency under the right conditions. For example, in Uganda the corruption level was so great that, for every $1 of government spending on education, only 20 cents reached the local primary schools targeted. Reforms that increased publicity (so that parents were aware of the money allocated) and improved monitoring raised this to 80 cents; not perfect, but an increase of 400%. This improvement does not, in itself, guarantee good education, but it is certainly an important factor in the equation. Unfortunately, such improvements cannot be achieved everywhere: in some cases decentralization can invite local corruption, particularly in hierarchical rural societies.

An example of using citizens to produce public benefits occurred in a pilot study in Nepal that gave local people direct control over a food-for-work program. It resulted in twice as many miles of roads being built with the same budget, a large part of which had previously been pocketed

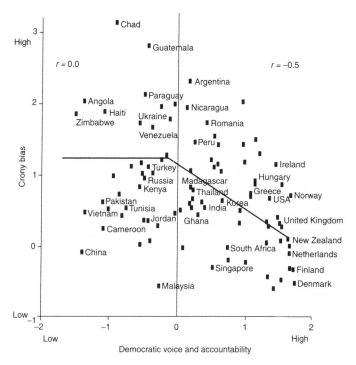

Figure 5.1. Crony bias, voice, and accountability
Note: Data from Executive Opinion survey (2003) and World Bank Institute's calculations; 'crony bias' is defined in the note to figure 6.3; the
voice and accountability variables are from Kaufmann, Kraay and Mastruzzi
(2003).
Source: Kaufmann (2004).

by the contractors rather than used to pay workers. However, a bid to extend this scheme met with resistance from
national officials and private contractors.

   In general, there seem to be two ways to limit corruption
via grassroots involvement: monitoring the use of central
funds and reporting misuse, or local provision of a service

under contract. To be effective, the service must first be wanted by the local community, the local organization must be relatively effective and egalitarian, and the relationship with national government must permit sustainable local empowerment.

However, such grassroots efforts are not sufficient in certain areas where monitoring by individuals is not practical; for example, procurement and revenue collection.

Opportunity 2: Procurement and civil service reform

Corruption in contracting occurs in every country, even in those at the high end of the honesty index. However, it is more widespread and harmful in some countries, particularly where the public sector accounts for a large share of construction contracts. Not only does corruption raise costs and reduce rates of return, it also offers little incentive for officials to make economically rational decisions. The result is often a double waste of money; for example, the wrong infrastructure projects are built, and they cost more than necessary.

Procurement reform offers the opportunity to rethink *what* the government buys, as well as *how* it makes the purchase. For example, buying standard goods sold in competitive markets reduces the risk of corruption compared with buying custom-made items. But this may not be possible for contracts such as large infrastructure projects. The World Bank requires the use of an International Competitive Bidding (ICB) process for its infrastructure loans.

This process might be supplemented with a benchmarking exercise in the form of a central database of contractors, including evidence on their efficiency and any involvement in fraud.

Alongside this, civil service reform can provide incentives for officials to avoid corruption – for example, by providing bonuses for meeting procurement targets, backed up by a credible enforcement effort. Unfortunately, such an approach would have little impact on "grand corruption," where senior politicians are implicated in procurement scandals.

Opportunity 3: Customs and tax administration

In the great majority of developing and transition countries where surveys have been conducted, customs and tax administration are cited as areas where large unofficial payments are common.

Collusion between corrupt officials, businesses, and individuals results in tax evasion, and the cost is borne by those taxpayers who are poorer or less well connected. In Pakistan, for instance, one study estimated that halving the losses due to corruption and mismanagement would increase the tax collected from 13.6% to over 15% of GDP. In Africa, the situation can be even worse: In the Gambia in the early 1990s, revenue from taxes and customs duties amounting to 8–9% of GDP was not collected. This represents six to seven times the amount the government spent on healthcare.

Corruption is often greatest where nominal tax rates are high. This can be addressed by reform which lowers overall tax rates, but levies taxes on bases that are difficult to hide or underestimate. For example, Russia recently introduced a flat rate of 13% for income tax, combined with credible enforcement measures, and tax revenues have now increased.

In cases where reform proves difficult, one option is to have tax assessment and collection carried out by a private firm, which then retains a percentage of the revenue. While this may be effective in the short term, it is an expensive option and only a first step toward a fully reformed local service.

Opportunity 4: Business regulation

In many countries illicit payments to ensure the introduction of particular rules and regulations, or the avoidance of existing ones, are common. This is not only a direct cost; corrupt firms also waste more time dealing with the authorities. Red tape and vague rules encourage this sort of corruption. A costless reform would therefore be to simplify the rules that make operation difficult, thereby reducing opportunities for bribery.

However, there are areas of regulation that are both complex and socially necessary, such as pollution control and worker health and safety. The key is to eliminate superfluous regulations and keep necessary ones, ensuring that they are administered in ways that minimize corruption opportunities. This can be facilitated by the expansion of diagnostic work being undertaken by the World Bank and other institutions to encourage efficient and honest systems of regulation.

Opportunity 5: International efforts

Several international treaties seeking to control corruption in multinational business have been enacted by bodies such as the Organization for Economic Cooperation and Development (OECD) and United Nations (UN). However, none of these can be effective without strong and effective policies in both the home and host countries.

The extractive industries sector illustrates some of the major issues. If the state is weak and corrupt, the presence of oil and other natural resources can actually hold back economic growth because attention is focused on personal gain by government officials rather than using the income stream for the public good. Proposals such as the international, multi-stakeholder Extractive Industries Transparency Initiative (EITI) seek to avoid this trap by encouraging both parties in transactions to publicly report payments.

Such initiatives have the potential to provide large benefits at minimal cost, but will be fiercely resisted by those who profit from current corruption. Equally, in countries with weak democratic institutions and poorly organized civil societies, leaders may find that transparency has little effect domestically.

A further aspect of international efforts is asset recovery, which forms an important part of the new UN treaty.

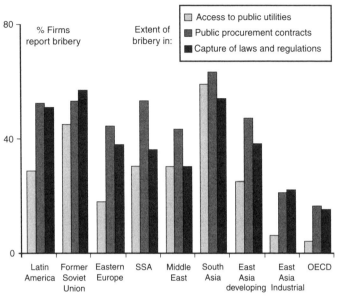

Figure 5.2. Unbundling corruption (Executive Opinion survey (GCR), regional averages, 2002)
Source: Kaufmann (2003).

However, this is a very difficult process, which would require controversial changes to entrenched legal regimes.

Summary of options for improving governance and reducing corruption

Corruption and poor governance in many developing countries are barriers to the effective tackling of poverty and other global challenges. The direct benefits of reform are difficult to assess but, since many reforms are essentially costless, cost effectiveness is likely to be very high.

A major challenge to reduction of corruption and poor governance is the difficulty of overcoming entrenched interests. A proportion of foreign aid should be directed to support institutional reform, even in countries judged presently to be so corrupt that they are not worth supporting. Isolation from the international community is only likely to make matter worse.

In summary, promising policy options are:

Option 1: Grassroots monitoring and service delivery, with technical assistance and information provision provided centrally by government or non-governmental organizations.

Option 2: Procurement reform via the development of benchmarks to reward efficient providers of public services.

Option 3: Reform of revenue collection through tax simplification, incentives to both tax collectors and payers, and monitoring.

Option 4: Reduction in the state-imposed costs of establishing and maintaining a business.

Option 5: International efforts to develop monitoring and transparency initiatives, as in the extractive industries.

THE CHALLENGE OF POOR GOVERNANCE AND CORRUPTION

OPPONENTS' VIEWS

Jean Cartier-Bresson and Jens Christopher Andvig have contributed their own detailed views on this challenge. Both agree with Susan Rose-Ackerman, author of the original paper, that corruption is a major challenge, but they put forward their own analyses of the causes, effects, and ways to tackle it.

Cartier-Bresson is in broad agreement with Rose-Ackerman's analysis, making the following points:

- Institutionalized corruption is a symptom of failing government and must be tackled by institutional reform.
- Realistic benefit-cost analysis is not possible, mainly because it is impractical to collect reliable data on what is essentially an illegal activity.
- Despite the general agreement among economists on the negative effects of corruption, there are formidable political barriers to overcome if governance is to be improved.

In his view, the key issues for discussion are the obstacles to good global governance and the difficulties of institutional reform. Various factors, including the end of the Cold War and the current round of globalization, have raised the profile of governance as an issue in recent years, but there are a number of reasons why comparatively little improvement has been made. In particular, there is a feeling among developing countries that reform is inequitable, with wealthier countries continuing to look after their own interests. Multinational companies, for example, may see little incentive to move away from ways of doing business that have served them well, and these companies are often strongly supported by their home governments.

This means that developing countries are unsure about how much assistance they will get with reform, or what share of the fruits of cooperation will be theirs. Reforming governments that are highly dependent on powerful interest groups is never easy, and strong incentives are needed if the effort is to be successsful. Effective reform of national governance is only likely to come about if global governance is first improved. In particular, international organizations must recognize that there are no universally applicable governance norms and that change is possible under any political regime.

Equally, there must be recognition that the transition to market democracy encouraged by international institutions is not only difficult and costly, but also politically suicidal for many authoritarian regimes. Dictators can foster genuine economic growth if they forgo short-term personal gain, whereas reforms can disadvantage some sectors of society. Democratization and liberalization also may themselves allow new forms of corruption to develop.

Success in tackling corruption can only come from balancing political realities with appropriate institutional reform. Although the reforms proposed by Rose-Ackerman are credible, their political feasibility is questionable.

Andvig, in his opponent paper, concentrates on just one of the opportunities in the challenge paper: international efforts to limit high-level corruption in business. However, first he discusses the difficulty of distinguishing perception of corruption from hard facts. He is clearly in agreement with Cartier-Bresson that reliable data is impossible to come by. In particular, he highlights the problem of "informational cascades": Statements on the degree of corruption are taken as true and repeated, even though there may be no hard evidence to support them.

He nevertheless agrees that corruption is a serious challenge, in particular where government is either itself dishonest or too weak to deal with corrupt institutions. In the absence of revolution or invasion, only relatively weak tools are available to deal with this. Some of these take the form of interventions from rich countries ("the North") to poorer, developing countries ("the South").

The first route for influence is via the behavior of multinational companies (MNCs), deemed to be ethical and honest in their home countries. Unfortunately, evidence from World Bank surveys is not encouraging: MNCs appear to act in much the same way as local companies in a corrupt business environment. Effort is needed to improve this situation. Punishing corruption by denying companies the right to bid for international contracts is one route, but must be strictly and fairly applied. Transparency initiatives as covered in the challenge paper also have their place, but voluntary agreements are not sufficient.

Foreign aid is another major route of influence. Denying it completely to dysfunctional states could, as Rose-Ackerman argues, have negative effects, but it could well be targeted to less corrupt sectors in a given country, or to projects under the control of international agencies. There is also a case for being more objective about where to target aid: use of corruption indices (however imperfect) and hard evidence is preferable to choice based on perceptions alone.

There are some aspects of aid which can actually promote corruption. In particular, wages for tasks performed by foreign aid agencies are often much higher than regular government pay.

In summary, while both authors are quite supportive of the challenge paper, they present rather pessimistic assessments of the outlook for improving governance and tackling corruption.

JERE R BEHRMAN[1], HAROLD ALDERMAN[2]
AND JOHN HODDINOTT[3]

6 Hunger and Malnutrition

Introduction: the challenge of hunger and malnutrition

Alongside the tragedy of acute famine, which is frequently shown on our televisions, there is a much bigger problem of chronic hunger and malnutrition in developing countries. Although this carries a very real human cost, it is the purpose of this chapter to look purely at the economic aspects: Assuring better nutrition can both reduce the economic drain on poor societies and help them become wealthier by increasing individuals' productivity.

This chapter reviews the nature and scale of the problem and the economic benefits that would flow from successful solutions. Four opportunity areas for effective

---

[1] William R Kenan Professor of Economics and Director of the Population Studies Center, University of Pennsylvania.
[2] Lead Human Development Economist in the Africa Region of the World Bank, Washington DC.
[3] Senior Research Fellow in the Food Consumption and Nutrition Division of the International Food Policy Research Institute, Washington DC.

95

use of resources to reduce malnutrition are then proposed:

1. Reducing the prevalence of Low Birth Weight.
2. Promotion of infant and child nutrition and exclusive breastfeeding.
3. Reducing the prevalence of iron deficiency anemia and vitamin A, iodine, and zinc deficiencies.
4. Investment in technology in developing country agriculture.

Using resources to address these opportunities would yield benefits greater than the cost, so these opportunities are economically justified. Benefits would, of course, also be realized on a wider social and human scale.

The nature of the challenge

Hunger has been described as "a condition in which people lack the basic food intake to provide them with the energy and nutrients for fully productive lives." Malnutrition, in its strict sense, can be associated with *over*-consumption of food, resulting for example in obesity, diabetes, or heart disease. Such problems are of increasing importance in some parts of the developing world. However, currently malnutrition in the developing world is primarily associated with *undernutrition*.

Although some commentators believe the regular figures published by the Food and Agriculture Organization of the United Nations (FAO) understate the true incidence of hunger, these nevertheless form the only relatively long-term global database. The figures indicate that the number of undernourished people in the developing world was 798 million in the 1999–2001 survey period: 17% of the total population of developing countries. Although this is an enormous problem, it should be seen against the background of their rapidly growing populations. There was an increase of 662 million people during the previous ten years (nearly twice the population of the 15-member European Union), while the number of chronically hungry people fell very slightly (by 18 million). Thus the prevalence of undernourishment has fallen substantially. 90% of these people live in the Asia-Pacific region (505 million) or sub-Saharan Africa (198 million). Despite the larger number of people affected overall, the trend in Asia-Pacific has been a reduction in the number and percentage of hungry people, primarily due to better nourishment of people in China. In Africa, on the other hand, the overall number of malnourished people increased, and in some countries the proportion of the affected population also rose.

The socio-economic breakdown of malnutrition has been estimated by the Hunger Task Force as approximately:

- 50% in farm households.
- 25% rural landless.
- 22% urban.
- 8% directly resource dependent (for instance, pastoralists and fishermen).

Development of a baby prior to birth (the gestational period) is crucial in determining its birth weight and affects childhood development. Mothers who are of small stature (directly affected by their own fetal development and childhood nutrition), poorly nourished and prone to endemic disease, tend to give birth to small children, who are at a developmental disadvantage. This is commonly measured by the incidence of Low Birth Weight (LBW), where an infant weighs less than 2500g at birth. In 2000, it was estimated that 16% of newborn babies in the developing world – 11.7 million children annually – could be classified as of LBW. In parts of south Asia, the situation is especially acute: an estimated 30% of babies are of LBW.

LBW is one important factor in determining early childhood development. Another is poor infant nutrition, particularly during the first two to three years of life. This has itself been linked to reduced breastfeeding. The net effect is reflected in the estimate that, in 2000, 162 million children (about one in three) were stunted.

In addition to the negative effect of malnutrition (both of the child and mother) on physical growth of children, deficiencies in micro-nutrients can have a major impact on development of intelligence. Lack of both iodine and iron has been implicated in impaired brain development, and this can affect enormous numbers of people: It is estimated that 2 billion people (one-third of the total global population) are affected by iodine deficiency, including 285 million six- to twelve-year-old children. In developing countries, it is estimated that 40% of children aged four and under suffer from anemia because of insufficient iron in their diets.

Potential benefits of meeting the challenge

Reduction of the incidence of malnutrition would have a number of benefits. The most important ones identified are:

- Reduction in infant mortality rates associated with LBW and deficiencies in micronutrients. The World Health Organisation (WHO) estimates that malnutrition contributed to 3.4 million child deaths in 2000; 60% of total child deaths. Reporting in 2001, a WHO commission estimated that a 10% increase in average life expectancy at birth results in an additional 0.3–0.4% of economic growth per year.
- Those who survive the effects of long-term malnutrition are more susceptible to disease, which further compromises their welfare. This also is a direct drain on health care services.
- Poor nutrition can directly affect physical productivity. Reduction in chronic hunger increases an individual's capacity to do physical work and increases his or her earning power. For example, a study of workers in rural Brazil reported that a 1% increase in height (associated with improved nutrition) leads to a 2–2.4% increase in wages or earnings.
- For a variety of reasons, childhood malnutrition often leads to an individual receiving less schooling, which translates directly into lower lifetime earnings for the people affected.

Opportunities related to hunger and malnutrition

Framework for considering opportunities

Although reduction in malnutrition would have clear economic benefits (in addition to human and social benefits), the purpose of the Copenhagen Consensus is to compare as objectively as possible these benefits with those delivered by meeting the other nine challenges.

This is done partly by comparing the overall net financial gain, which may sound relatively straightforward but is complicated by the fact that benefits accrue in many cases over long periods (the remaining lifetimes of children whose nutrition is improved, for example). To bring all projects to a common basis, an estimate must be made of the *current* value of all benefits to be received in the future. This is done by a process called *discounting*, which is simply an assumption of the future value of money compared with that of today. However, the choice of a particular discount rate will, over a period of ten years or more, make an enormous difference to the current value (what economists call the Present Discounted Value). Indeed, it can make the difference between an opportunity being seen as highly valuable and being rejected as having too small economic benefit to warrant the cost. There are other problems in making such estimates as well. Putting aside the question of discounting, for example, it is difficult to estimate the impacts of interventions given imperfect data that generally is generated by individuals' behaviours and it often is difficult to estimate costs given programs that bundle interventions and use accounting prices that differ from marginal scarcity prices. Finally, for the efficiency motive for public subsidies what is needed are differences between private and social rates of returns, but such estimates are difficult to make and rarely available.

In a nutshell, there are no easy answers that are likely to be universally applicable. It is expected that a more subtle

Table 6.1. Summary of benefits and costs for opportunities related to Hunger and Malnutrition

Opportunities and targeted populations	Benefits ($)	Costs ($)	Benefits-costs ratio ($)	Discount rates (%)
Treatments for women with asymptomatic bacterial infections	$580–986	$200–2000	0.58–4.93	3–5%
Breastfeeding promotion in hospitals in which norm has been promotion of use of infant formula	$131–134	$133–1064	4.80–7.35	3–5%
Vitamin A (pre child under six years)	$37–43	$1–10	4.3–43	3–5%
Dissemination of new cultivars with higher yield potential			8.8–14.7	3–5%

analysis of costs and benefits at a country level – and their sensitivity to variables – would be necessary.

Opportunity 1: Reducing the prevalence of Low Birth Weight

Some 12 million children in the developing world are born each year weighing less than 2500g, and are classified as Low Birth Weight. Increases in the proportion of babies of normal birth weight would have multiple benefits. In particular:

- Saving lives. Although placing a monetary value on human life is uniquely difficult, it has to be done to make an economic comparison. One method, used here, is to use the resource costs of alternative means of saving a life.
- Reducing costs of caring for newborn babies in hospital.
- Reducing health care costs for surviving LBW babies, who have a higher incidence of illness than heavier babies.
- Improved lifetime productivity, based both on better physical development by adulthood and longer schooling/better learning ability.
- Reducing costs of chronic diseases associated with LBW.
- Benefits to following generations. LBW mothers themselves give birth to small babies, continuing the cycle of disadvantage.

Taking all these into account, it has been estimated that the current value of actions that would result in one birth of a normal weight baby who would otherwise be LBW is $580. Over half of this comes from increased productivity over the child's lifetime. This means that interventions that cost less than $580 per child affected would be justified in purely economic terms.

A range of relatively simple, and in many cases inexpensive, actions has been suggested. These include provision

of antibiotics and anti-parasitics, insecticide-treated bed-
nets to reduce malaria incidence and supply of iron/folate
dietary supplements. For example, it costs $2 per patient to
supply antibiotics to Ugandan women with sexually transmitted diseases. As well as the direct benefits of curing disease, for every hundred women treated, two cases of LBW
are prevented: a cost of $100 per case. Since each normal
birth of an otherwise underweight baby is worth $580, this
has a benefit-cost ratio of 5.8.

In another study, dietary supplements of iron and folate
for pregnant women in Nepal prevented one case of LBW
for every 11 women treated. The cost of treatment in a large-
scale program is estimated as $13 per patient, or less than
$150 for each LBW birth prevented: a benefit-cost ratio of
about 4. Of course, such interventions may also be justifiable on other grounds.

The key point with Opportunity 1 is that a number of
interventions have been shown to decrease the incidence
of LBW at a cost that is far below the estimated value of
the benefit received. This means that such initiatives are
readily justifiable, even with significant changes to some of
the assumptions made in the calculations.

Opportunity 2: Improving infant and child nutrition and exclusive breastfeeding promotion

Nutrition in the first two years of life is second only to
development in the womb in determining a child's healthy
growth. Promoting breastfeeding in communities where

incomes are low and food and water supplies are often contaminated can have significant benefits for childhood development and lifetime productivity. The gains are supplementary to those of Opportunity 1 and of a similar magnitude. Costs of effective programs in place already make such actions easily justifiable in economic terms. For example, studies conducted in Latin American hospitals show benefit-cost ratios for breast feeding promotion of about 4 for typical interventions. Community-based growth promotion is also a promising intervention in some environments.

Opportunity 3: Reducing the prevalence of iron deficiency anemia and iodine, vitamin A, and zinc deficiencies

Lack of iron not only has an influence on fetal and childhood development (and thus, for example, has a significant effect on the number of small babies born) but also has a direct negative effect on the productivity of adults.

Iodine intake also is an important factor in determining birth weight. In addition, lack of iodine in childhood reduces brain development: A study has shown, for example, that iodine-deficient individuals score an average of 13.5 points lower in IQ tests.

Vitamin A deficiency can permanently damage eyesight, even causing blindness. Dietary supplements not only decrease the incidence of blindness in children but also reduce deaths and the severity of some illnesses. The direct benefits associated with the (relatively inexpensive) provision of vitamin A supplements are mainly in terms of this second category, reducing childhood mortality, but there is also a productivity gain during the lifetime of workers who would otherwise have been blind.

The benefits of zinc supplementation are to be seen in reduced LBW and improved physical development in childhood.

Delivery of additional micronutrients can be by a variety of routes. Flour fortification, supplementation with tablets, vitamin A as an addition to immunization programs, or even boosting iron by supply of iron cooking pots can all be cost effective ways of improving nutrition. Dietary interactions are complex, but an adequate supply of important vitamins and minerals can make an important contribution to well being at various stages of an individual's life. As an example, many studies have been done on vitamin A supplementation and it has been shown to be one of the most cost-effective medical interventions known, with a benefit-cost ratio of over 140.

Opportunity 4: Investment in technology in developing country agriculture

In an ideal world, all necessary nutrition should be obtainable from a readily-available, balanced diet. This opportunity therefore focuses on developing improved seed varieties and agricultural practices that can enable people to grow higher and more consistent yields of more nutritious food. This is not just a case of subsistence farmers growing more to eat: rather it is a question of more productive farming which gives farmers a better return on their investment, increases demand for the labor of landless people, and reduces the price of food to make it more accessible to both rural and urban populations.

The "green revolution" of the 1960s and '70s is a clear example of how modern plant breeding advances can be widely employed for the benefit of the poor. In this case, high-yielding dwarf varieties of rice and wheat have vastly increased the supply of staple foods in Asia and South America. Similar advances could be derived using the best technologies available now, including biotechnological advances.

Returns on investment in this area are difficult to estimate accurately, but studies have shown that the relatively modest up-front costs of plant breeding can be quickly recouped, and that the benefits continue to accrue for many years until the seeds are displaced by the use of new varieties giving even higher benefits. Calculations on the economics of new cultivars with higher concentrations of micronutrients (for example, vitamin A precursor in "golden rice") indicate that benefit-cost ratios can be very high – in the region of 15–20 – even with very conservative assumptions on uptake and effectiveness. Investment in agricultural technologies is the single most effective means of increasing the incomes of those groups in the developing world who suffer from chronic hunger.

Conclusions

Taking up the opportunities presented here would make a major contribution to the welfare of the world's poorest people – the 800 million who are chronically undernourished. Although this can be regarded as a good in itself, the clear evidence is that all of the approaches described are also economically justified in the sense that the projected benefits outweigh the costs.

HUNGER AND MALNUTRITION
OPPONENTS' VIEWS

The two opponent papers on hunger and malnutrition do not question the basic analysis and opportunities proposed by Behrman, Alderman and Hoddinott in their challenge paper. Instead, in rather different ways, they provide more discussion and insights to support the case for tackling this challenge.

Simon Appleton believes that Berhman et al have made a very thorough and rigorous assessment of the problem and proposed some important policy opportunities. While acknowledging that it is a very broad issue, what he sees missing in the paper is some discussion of how to reduce poverty, which is intimately associated with malnutrition. He also notes that famine is not dealt with, and wonders whether famine relief might not be the basis for a fifth opportunity.

Appleton suggests that the challenge paper authors may have underestimated the benefits of reducing hunger, first by only considering the direct costs of malnutrition and second by not including non-nutritional benefits (e.g., increased welfare of mothers treated to reduce the incidence of Low Birth Weight). However, Behrman et al were asked to address a very specific topic, and were probably quite justified in trying to keep a narrow focus.

Another criticism is that no weighting is given to where the benefits are received: In general, a given benefit will have a greater impact on those most in need. Taking this into account, the third opportunity – micronutrient supplementation – should be given a higher priority because vitamin and mineral deficiencies are concentrated in the poorest sections of society. More generally, Appleton suggests that the challenge of hunger and malnutrition should be given higher priority than challenges which are less connected with poverty, such as financial or trade liberalization.

In Appleton's opinion, the challenge paper also puts too low a monetary value on lives saved. Valuing life is always very difficult, and there is a case for considering lives saved in a separate category from economic benefits when prioritizing challenges. In any case, this factor also contributes to an underestimation of the benefits afforded by the opportunities.

To set against this, the authors have used rather fragmentary and partial evidence to support their findings, for example, by extrapolating data from the USA and UK to developing countries. This gives the benefit-cost ratios a greater level of uncertainty, but there is no apparent systematic over- or underestimation.

The final point made by Appleton is that benefit-cost ratios are quoted for a number of individual interventions, but there is no aggregate ratio for each opportunity. This he believes is necessary if the Copenhagen Consensus experts are to be able to prioritize the challenges properly. He therefore makes his own benefit-cost ratio estimates as follows:

1. Reducing the prevalence of Low Birth Weight   4
2. Improving infant and child nutrition   3
3. Reducing micro-nutrient deficiencies   36
4. Agricultural research and development   15

Peter Svedberg takes a very different approach in his commentary. In his words, Behrman and co-authors "exude optimism" about coping with childhood malnutrition. He also believes there are further causes for optimism: availability of cheaper and better medicines and better targeting of combined nutrition and health programs. Any interventions that improve health also will certainly have a beneficial effect on nutrition.

Svedberg shares Appleton's views on the intimate links between malnutrition and poverty. He looks at length at the empirical evidence, noting, for example, that over half the variation in childhood stunting between countries is accounted for by differences in income. Richer households not only have the money to feed themselves better, they also provide more revenue to governments that can be used to alleviate hunger.

He goes further in trying to understand the root causes of hunger in developing countries, noting that there are significant differences in the extent of malnutrition between countries with the same income per head. His conclusion is that it is institutional and infrastructure problems that fail to deliver new treatments to those in need: there must be effective channels and trained personnel for these to be delivered.

The lack of effective infrastructure can be compounded by endemic corruption. Many of the countries with the worst malnutrition problems score very low on the corruption index published by Transparency International (an NGO). These low scores represent "deep-rooted and widespread corruption at most levels of society." Under these circumstances, even well-targeted programs are unlikely to succeed. Even worse is the political indifference shown by some regimes to the suffering of their people.

Overall, Svedberg is much more pessimistic than Behrman et al about likely progress in meeting this challenge in the short- to medium term. He thinks there is little hope of meeting the Millennium Development Goal of halving the prevalence of child under-nutrition over the next ten years. This view highlights the degree of interrelationship of many of the challenges: Programs have a low chance of success unless the country targeted is peaceful and not corrupt, and sustained, long-term improvement will not occur without significant progress being made in poverty reduction.

PHILIP MARTIN[1]

7 Population and Migration

Description of the challenge

For most of human history, migration has been constrained by physical barriers and transport difficulties rather than government action. More recently, sharply different rates of population and economic growth across the world have combined to make many workers from poorer countries eager to move to countries where more jobs are available and wages are much higher. Modern communications make the differences even more visible, and modern transport makes migration easy and affordable. But migrants are not always welcome in rich countries.

In an ideal world, such economically motivated migration would benefit migrants, increase global GDP and promote economic convergence between rich and poor countries. After a time, this would reduce the pressure to migrate. The challenge addressed in this chapter is ensuring that the migration that occurs promotes equality.

---

[1] University of California, Davis.

Global economic convergence is a goal supported by most economists and other commentators. However, there is no consensus on how migration might achieve this, with strong arguments being made both for and against.

In 2000, it was estimated that 175 million people – 3% of the global population – were migrants who had lived outside their country of birth or citizenship for a year or more. This number had doubled in the previous 25 years, during which the world's population grew by 50%. Most migrants move from poorer to richer countries, with about 60% of the total now living in the more developed countries. Although there are many more potential migrants, immigration has become a major political issue in receiving countries (for example, European Union Member States). Public opinion polls suggest that most residents oppose further immigration and support government measures to reduce illegal or irregular migration.

Most economists welcome migration from lower- to higher-wage countries, because it uses resources more efficiently and maximizes production. The global economic gain is the sum of net income gains of individual migrants, plus a small bonus for receiving countries. It was estimated in 1984 that world GDP could more than double if free migration was allowed, adding between $5 trillion and $16 trillion to the 1977 figure of $8 trillion. The global economy has now grown to over $30 trillion, making potential gains today far greater. With such potential gains, the benefit from even partial liberalization of labor flows could benefit the world economy far more than trade liberalization.

For countries receiving migrant workers, the overall economic impacts are clearly positive, albeit there will be some

Table 7.1. Europe and Africa, demography, 1800–2050

	Share of world population %		
	1800	2000	2050
Africa	8	13	20
Europe	20	12	7
World pop. (bn)	1	6	9

losers who must be compensated. For countries that are net senders of migrants, the situation is less clear-cut. So, although the global economy and individual migrants may benefit, sending countries may find their economic development held back by the loss of talented, educated citizens. In a worst-case scenario, migration may actually cause further divergence of per capita incomes.

There are clear arguments for developed countries, with aging populations and fewer young workers, to use immigration to stabilize work forces. Many developing countries are happy to export some of their excess labor to increase remittances and acquire new skills. However, managing migration optimally for the benefit of all parties is more difficult.

Migration is driven by differences. As economic differences widen, developing country populations continue to grow, and transport becomes cheaper and easier, migration pressures will increase. As well as the basic gap in GDP, the continued drift of labor away from agriculture (the world's major employer) creates a larger pool of willing migrants. This is partly a result of trade barriers to agricultural produce, which reduce farm employment in poor countries. At the same time, there is a demand for migrant labor to work on the subsidized, protected farms in industrialized countries.

Ethnic or security differences also drive migration. Conflict and the creation of new nations in the old Communist bloc have caused population shifts and contributed to the flow of migrants, for example.

Assessing the opportunities

Many countries receiving migrants are attempting to manage immigration by discouraging potential migrants through tighter controls and restriction of benefits. However, this is not an optimal solution.

Three opportunities are assessed in this chapter, all of which could be implemented in the next 5 to 15 years. These would each raise the benefits and reduce the costs of migration, most of which would probably occur in any case. In brief, these are:

- Active selection systems to allow in those foreigners who are most likely to succeed. This would reduce fears of immigration and allow wider entry channels to be opened for skilled workers and professionals.
- Widening legal entry channels for unskilled guest workers, together with encouragement to return to their countries of origin. This would provide temporary labor without permanent settlement.
- Using the 3 R's of migration – recruitment, remittances, and returns – to promote economic convergence over time.

The overall goal is to create a world in which migration is unnecessary because sufficient opportunity exists at home. The majority of people do not migrate, and they will only enjoy higher incomes if their countries prosper. The challenge is to ensure that the migration of the exceptional few also improves conditions for those who stay behind.

Opportunity 1: Active selection procedures for migrants

Whereas migration at one time was a difficult, expensive, and usually permanent process, the situation today is much more fluid. Migrants now select their destinations and often adjust to long-term resident status after entering on a temporary basis. This adjustment process can be difficult and frustrating for them, and the ambiguity of status of many arrivals often leads to the perception or fear of excessive immigration in the host country. Active selection procedures could improve this situation, for the benefit of all concerned.

We have already seen that the net economic effect of immigration to industrialized countries is positive but small. More migration might be tolerated by the host country's native residents if those migrants who are likely to generate maximum economic benefits to the destination country are selected. This is the approach successfully adopted in Canada, which uses a points-based decision system covering factors such as education and language skills. The country has continuing high levels of immigration (approximately a quarter of a million people annually into a population of 32 million) and significant public satisfaction with the policy.

Alternatively, demand-based systems can be adopted, so that employers select migrants they believe best suited for jobs on offer. This inevitably creates tensions between companies wishing to employ foreigners and the need to protect local workers. To ensure the local labor pool is properly searched, employers could be required to pay a fee to employ migrants.

There are two potential downsides to selection procedures:

1. The already high costs of curbing unwanted and unlawful immigration may rise, to ensure that all immigration is properly managed and controls are not bypassed. In 2002, Canada, Germany, the Netherlands, the UK, and the USA collectively spent at least $17 billion to enforce immigration law and care for asylum seekers (about two-thirds of the amount they spent on overseas aid).
2. Selecting the brightest and best from developing countries could increase inequality and migration pressures. Some compensatory mechanism such as exit taxes or continued taxation of migrants by their countries of origin might alleviate this.

Bearing in mind these provisos, increased immigration of well-educated, productive workers to developed countries could help to stabilize their work forces and pension systems. Resistance from the native populations is likely to decrease as these benefits become apparent. There is also a plausible argument that a certain level of "brain drain" would be beneficial for developing countries. If people believe that migration could increase their returns from education, more people will work for higher qualifications, and only a proportion of them will emigrate. The pool of well-educated nationals will increase even as the brain drain continues.

Although managed migration can be beneficial for all parties, it is not always so. At one end of the spectrum, migration of IT specialists from India has contributed to a virtuous circle of increased technical education and the growth of a significant computer services industry in India itself. At the other end, emigration of doctors and nurses from South Africa has contributed to a continuing decline in the number of healthcare professionals available at a time of increasing need.

Developing countries, led by India, want to see liberalization of the temporary movement of workers (initially professionals, later unskilled) on a global basis. The mechanism for this in the long run would be a visa issued under the General Agreement on Trade in Services (GATS, part of the World Trade Organisation).

Opportunity 2: Guest worker policies

Alongside the managed immigration of highly skilled workers, guest worker programs aim to add mostly unskilled workers temporarily to the labor forces of developed countries. They usually do so-called "3D" jobs (dirty, dangerous, and difficult) for which local labor is not available.

However, such programs generally have not been a complete success. They have led to both labor market distortions (where employers rely on a continued supply of immigrant labor) and dependence (when migrants and their families depend long-term on earnings from foreign jobs). There has been little large-scale resumption of the process in recent years, but if better ways could be found to manage guest workers, there would be benefits for both workers and employers.

In the 1960s, millions of guest workers from Southern Europe and North Africa were employed temporarily in Western Europe and were regarded as hardworking. However, when recruitment stopped in 1973–74, many unemployed workers chose not to return to their countries of origin. It became easier for new arrivals to receive welfare benefits than get jobs, and migrants began to be viewed by many native residents as a drain on society.

New guest worker programs set up in the 1990s were much more focused, targeting single groups such as computer programmers or farm laborers. At the same time, there are now far more irregular foreign workers in developed countries. They can be encouraged into short-term legal employment by appropriate tax and subsidy regimes.

The labor market distortion inherent in large-scale guest worker schemes can be reduced by appropriate use of employer-paid taxes and fees. Dependence can be tackled by use of incentives such as repayment of migrant workers' social security payments when they return to their countries of origin.

Significant expansion of temporary worker migration still presents challenges. In particular, enforcement becomes a major burden, especially when some sectors have large numbers of illegal workers. One solution is "earned legalization," whereby irregular workers can earn legal status by registering and completing employment and tax requirements.

Although economic incentives can help host countries to manage temporary migrants, their effect is not always predictable. For example, migrant families were encouraged to leave Germany in the early 1980s by the offer of a departure bonus of up to $5,000 and repayment of their social security contributions. Between 1982 and 1984–5, there was a net loss of 300,000 of the then 4.7 million foreigners, but it was concluded afterward that the majority of foreigners who took the departure bonus would have left in any case. Of course, from the perspective of returnees, the bonus was a significant benefit, but apparently not an incentive.

Detailed examination of the economic impact on the USA as a host country showed that workers who competed with migrants tended to move away from the area, dissipating the impact across the country. While the average wage reduction due to immigration over the 1980–2000 period was 3.2%, this rose to almost 9% for US-born workers who had not completed high school.

In summary, making the transition from the current widespread employment of illegal workers to a world of legal migrants is a very difficult challenge given growing international inequality.

Opportunity 3: Migration for development

Development should reduce economically motivated migration by eliminating its root causes. Migration can speed up this process if the 3Rs of recruitment, remittances, and returns accelerate economic growth in the country of origin. However, the current impacts of migration are less clear in poor countries than in receiving countries.

Recruitment of skilled professionals from developing countries could reduce economic growth in these countries. However, remittances both from both skilled and unskilled migrants, and encouragement of returns, can be managed to promote rather than hinder economic growth.

Remittances can be maximized if developing countries set realistic exchange rates and adopt economic policies likely to foster growth. These remittances more than doubled in the ten years from the late 1980s, overtaking official Overseas Development Aid (ODA) by 1997. In 2001, the total amount remitted was over $70 billion, compared to just over $50 billion of ODA.

Half of all remittances are to India, Mexico, the Philippines, Morocco, Egypt, and Turkey, but they can also be particularly important to smaller and island nations (for example they are, 37% of GDP in Tonga and 26% in Lesotho). The money sent improves the lives of people in receiving households, but also benefits the local economy via multiplier effects.

Skilled returnees can help to establish new industries, for example, the high-tech sectors in Taiwan, India, and

Table 7.2. Migration: Economic impacts, 2001 data

Countries	World	Low	Middle	High
Population (m)	6,133	2,511	2,667	955
Ave GDP($/year)	5,140	430	1,850	26,710
Total GDP ($bn)	31,500	1,069	4,922	25,506
Moving 100 million people from low to high, same				
***per capita* averages**				
Population (m)		2,411		1,055
Ave GDP($/year)	5,566	430		26,710
Total GDP ($bn)	34,138	1,037		28,179
GDP%	8			
Moving 10 million people from low to high, same				
***per capita* averages**				
Population (m)		2,501		965
Ave GDP($/year)	5,706	430		26,710
Total GDP ($bn)	31,760	1,065		25,773
Change in ave/tot GDP (%)	1			

Source: World Bank and own calculations

China. China sent 580,000 students overseas between 1979 and 1999, of which 25% had returned by 2002.

Policies that encourage migration for development purposes (and, in the longer term, reduce international labor movements) will inevitably cause a short-term increase in migration. This can lead to resistance in receiving countries, slowing the economic integration needed to accelerate development, so careful management is necessary.

Development can also be fostered by trade liberalization. For instance, countries that wish to reduce migration pressures could do so by no longer protecting their uncompetitive agricultural industries. Currently, industrial countries spend over $300 billion annually in farming subsidies (six times the amount spent on ODA). Unrestricted access to world markets for agricultural commodities would raise developing country GDPs by 5%, compared to the average 1% gain from remittances.

Conclusions

Global GDP is increased by the higher incomes received by most migrant workers. Receiving countries also receive a small net benefit to their economies. Countries of origin benefit significantly from remittances and, in some cases, the return of migrants to their native land.

The benefits of migration (higher incomes) are immediate and easy to see; the costs are delayed and very difficult to estimate. However, many people in host countries perceive the cost to be high. Tackling this perception through the proposed opportunities for better management of migration would allow the realization of greater benefits of migration to the global economy, the receiving countries, and countries of origin. In the longer term, properly managed migration would be an important tool to reduce inequalities between countries. Lowering barriers to migration should rank very high on the global list of challenges.

POPULATION: MIGRATION

Contrasting views of Philip Martin's challenge paper are given in these two opposition papers. Roger Böhning is in broad agreement with the analysis and recommendations, differing mainly on the roles the State must play if the proposals are to work and in believing that a World Migration Organization could play a useful role. Mark Rosenzweig, on the other hand, is quite critical of Martin's analysis. Together, these critiques provide interesting new insights into the challenge presented by migration.

Böhning considers what must be done by the State to make what Martin describes as the "transition from the current widespread employment of irregular workers to a world of legal migrants." His first point is that labor inspection regimes are at their weakest (essentially non-existent) in the "informal" employment sector, where illegal employment is common. Secondly, he sees a link between illegal migration and corruption, in both the home and receiving countries. Thirdly, since State recruitment of migrants has effectively stopped in most countries, the vacuum has largely been filled by intermediaries supplying illegal workers. All three factors require attention if migration is to be managed properly.

Turning to Martin's proposal to attract skilled workers while compensating the home countries for the brain drain, Böhning sees a good case for selection by educational qualification to be put on European policy agendas, and sees this as far preferable to promoting immigration as a demographic quick fix to the problems presented by an ageing population. This encouragement of selective immigration, together with capping numbers of refugees accepted, is unlikely to be politically acceptable in many countries for the foreseeable future. The other aspect of this proposal – compensation of home countries – he sees as unrealistic in practice. Promoting it as a possibility is therefore unfair.

The point where Böhning takes issue with Martin is his second opportunity: encouragement of temporary guest workers. He believes that this would ultimately create a larger problem of illegal migration, and it is better to consider all migrant workers as being in the receiving country on a permanent basis. To make the policy work, labor inspections would be needed in the informal sector to remove illegal immigrants, and the practice of regularizing the status of illegals after a certain length of time (responsible for a high proportion of legal immigration admissions) would need to be stopped in all but exceptional cases.

Böhning accepts the point that managed migration – including regular remittances and a proportion of returnees – can help with economic development. This process could be helped by the proposed establishment of a World Migration Organisation (WMO), but setting objectives that are acceptable to all parties would be a challenge. In general, receiving countries would object to the promotion of greater levels of migration, which might be favored by some sending countries. However, fighting unlawful migration, encouraging cross-border cooperation to manage flows, and devising an equitable system for sharing migrant workers' taxes between sending and receiving countries would form a worthwhile basis for the constitution of a WMO.

Rosenzweig takes a more critical view of the challenge paper. His first objection is to the way the global benefits of migration have been calculated. Martin makes low assumptions about the wages of migrants in their home countries, so exaggerating the increased income they receive in the host countries. Even for the group with the lowest skills, home country wages have been understated by about a half. His use of average figures also hides the fact that higher-skilled immigrants each make a larger gross contribution to the global economy than the lower-skilled. This is an argument for greater migration of skilled workers, but not for increased migration across the board. The revised calculations suggest that increasing migration by one million low-skilled workers would contribute $8 billion to the world economy; for the same number of college graduates, the contribution would be $17 billion.

On the question of remittances and their contribution to developing country economies, Rosenzweig believes Martin's figures to be overstated. Research shows that remittances average only 4% of earnings of US immigrants. However, these amounts are still significant for the home country, increasing country income by 7–11%.

Return of some emigrants to their home countries represents a real gain to these countries, and appears to be happening in significant numbers. A survey conducted in the USA in 2003, for example, showed that 21% of male immigrants with employment visas expected not to live in America in the long term.

Rosenzweig is sceptical about the value of education-based selection systems. Supportive family networks seem effective in migration success, and most legal immigration in the US is sponsored by American citizens. Finally, he sees no merit in encouraging temporary migration. This would expand the population of unassimilated migrants with little incentive to learn the host country language. Such an approach offers no advantages over the encouragement of all legal migration to be permanent in principle. This gives immigrants incentives to settle and integrate, but in practice a proportion will also return to heir home country, taking useful skills with them.

Both opponents agree on the desirability of managing migration properly. In particular, they believe all immigration should be on the same basis: permanent in principle. However, neither makes a strong case for this particular challenge to be considered a high priority by the Copenhagen Consensus conference.

FRANK RIJSBERMAN[1]

8 The Water Challenge

Characteristics of the water challenge

Despite the massive investment in water resource development during the twentieth century – in recent decades also reaching the developing world – there is still what many see as a "water crisis." This has two key facets:

- Lack of access to safe and affordable domestic water supply (for over a billion people) and sanitation (for nearly half the world's population).
- Lack of access to water for productive purposes for the rural poor.

There is clearly sufficient water available in the world for all mankind's needs: domestic, industrial, and agricultural, although it is distributed very unevenly. The problem is not lack of water, but that the unserved do not have access to capital (financial or political) to make it available to them.

[1] Director General, International Water Management Institute, Colombo, Sri Lanka.

129

The challenge addressed here is, therefore, providing access for poor people to safe water for domestic and productive purposes.

Domestic water needs are relatively small; only 20–50 litres per head each day in developing countries (although up to ten times this in the USA and Europe). In contrast, each person needs thousands of litres a day to produce their food. About 1,000 litres (one cubic metre) of water are needed to produce one kilogram of cereal grain, and meat production requires considerably higher quantities. On average, each person needs seventy times as much water to feed them as for all domestic purposes.

Water resources are subject to competition for different uses, particularly agriculture and the environment. Large development projects have, in the worst cases, led to rivers running dry and to enormous depletion of aquifers. This challenge therefore has two crucial dimensions: service delivery to those people without adequate water supplies and sustainable resource management.

The case for government involvement in water

In both historical and modern times, water service provision has generally been seen as a government responsibility. This is largely because water is regarded as a public good and its availability as a basic human right, best administered by the public sector. However, the cost of service provision has to be borne somewhere, and an emotional argument continues as to whether individual citizens should pay at least part of the cost of providing the water they consume, whether to public or private providers.

The experience of poor returns from centralized water infrastructure projects has shown that these are best managed at local government or community level. This leads to greater involvement of the users and better accountability. There is now a general trend toward decentralization of service provision and introduction of water charges.

There are also arguments that governments are not the best providers of services such as water supply. Experience in France and the UK, for example, shows that private companies can also successfully carry out this role within a government regulatory framework. Nevertheless, there is still a strong case for public investment if it can be better targeted at poor communities to reduce poverty and hunger and improve public health rather than just being a narrow, technology-based approach to water provision.

The costs of managing water badly

What costs does the current water crisis impose on society? The 2003 report from the United Nations (UN) Task Force on Water and Sanitation gives some sense of the scale of the problem, for example:

- Nearly half the population of the developing world is suffering at any given time from diseases related to poor access to clean water and sanitation, ranging from diarrhoea to a number of parasitic illnesses.

- Over two billion people are infected with water- or soil-borne parasitic diseases (bilharzias and helminthes), with 300 million suffering serious illness.
- Well-designed water and sanitation infrastructure reduces the incidence of bilharzias by more than three-quarters.
- A range of pollutants also affects health; high arsenic levels in water from deep wells affects 50 million people in Asia.

Diarrhoeal diseases are the greatest health problem, with more than four billion cases and between one and two million deaths each year. The total burden of diseases associated with poor quality water, sanitation and hygiene has been assessed as 82 million Disability Adjusted Life Years (DALYs) annually. Taking a low valuation of $500 per DALY, the economic cost amounts to $40 billion (considerably more if the higher DALY valuations used by authors of other challenge papers are used).

Moving on to water for agricultural use, it is found that there is a strong correlation between rural poverty and low levels of irrigated land. Irrigation is clearly an important tool for poverty reduction. But, where land distribution is inequitable, the benefits of irrigation are also delivered unequally.

In India, irrigation has become more widely available to marginal farmers via privately pumped groundwater, made available cheaply because of current electricity subsidies. However, the lack of control of groundwater exploitation has led to severe depletion of major aquifers.

Further development of small-scale irrigation technology – drip and micro-sprinkler systems, for example – can repay a small farmer's investment very quickly. This enables water resources to be used more productively.

Appropriate provision of water can be a key opportunity for reduction of rural poverty. The provision has to be done with due regard to environmental factors to avoid potential large remedial costs in the longer term. Irrigated land is prone to water-logging and salinization, leading to reduced productivity. It is estimated that 30% of irrigated land already suffers from reduced productivity, but no remediation opportunities have been identified yielding benefits on the scale comparable to those reviewed in this chapter.

The economic literature on the benefits of improved water management is rather sparse, with many projects in the sector based primarily on a human rights approach. Nevertheless, this chapter examines the challenge from an economic perspective.

Water opportunities

Two key opportunities to meet the challenge are discussed more fully below, but there are several others which should also be noted:

- *Re-using waste water for peri-urban agriculture*. Installation of low-cost sewerage in medium to large cities in developing countries could provide biologically safe irrigation water for poor farmers living in the slums and shanty towns at the city's margins. This would not only have a direct benefit for the farmers, but also prevent pollution from untreated waste water.

- *Developing sustainable smallholder agriculture in wetlands*. As an alternative to complete reclamation, some wetlands (for example, "dambos" in Africa) can be adapted for agriculture while maintaining the existing ecosystem. Only a relatively small number of farmers would be directly affected, but there would be significant benefits associated with maintenance of the environmental services of the wetlands.
- *Research to increase the productivity of water for food production*. More efficient water use can meet the rapid increase in urban and industrial water demands without further environmental impact. Investment costs are relatively low, at $300–400 billion over 10–15 years, and expected benefits are high; benefit-cost ratios of 15–20 have been estimated.

Although presented as discrete options, these can also be components of an integrated approach to water supply, together with the two options explored in more detail below.

Opportunity 1: Community-managed low-cost water supply and sanitation

This option covers an integrated package of measures designed, implemented, and managed with the full involvement of the community. Low-cost water supply would entail the provision of standpipes and low-cost sanitation would comprise good-quality latrines in rural areas and low-cost sewerage in urban areas (septic tanks or shallow, small-bore

Table 8.1. Number of people, in millions, to whom access must be extended by 2015 in order to meet MDG targets

Regions/Country categories	Number of people to gain access to improved water supply by 2015			Number of people to gain access to improved sanitation by 2015		
	Urban	Rural	Total	Urban	Rural	Total
SSA	175	184	359	178	185	363
Middlle East and North Africa	104	30	134	105	34	140
South Asia	243	201	444	263	451	714
East Asia and Pacific	290	174	465	330	376	705
Latin America and Caribbean	121	20	141	132	29	161
CEE/CIS and Baltic States	27	0	27	24	0	
Total	961	609	1,570	1,032	1,076	2,108

Source: UN Task Force on Water and Sanitation (2003, 47).

sewerage plus low-cost treatment). These would be supplemented by hygiene education.

At the end of the twentieth century, it was estimated that 1.1 billion people did not have access to a safe water supply, and 2.4 billion people were not served by basic sanitation. One of the Millennium Development Goals (MDGs) is to halve these numbers by 2015, which means not only halving the present numbers, but also catering for a significant population increase.

To achieve this goal, just over 1.5 billion extra people would have to be supplied with safe water, about 60% of them in urban communities. In the case of sanitation, the figure is 2.1 billion people, this time split quite evenly

Table 8.2. Improved versus non-improved water supply and sanitation

	Improved	Non-improved
Water supply	• Household connection • Public standpipe • Borehole • Protected dug well • Protected spring water • Rainwater collection	• Unprotected well • Unprotected spring • Vendor-provided water • Bottled water[a] • Tanker-truck provided
Sanitation	• Connection to a public sewer • Connection to a septic system • Pour-flush latrine • Simple pit latrine • Ventilated improved pit latrine	• Service or bucket latrines[b] • Public latrines • Latrines with open pit

[a] Considered as 'non-improved' because of quantity rather than quality of supplied water.
[b] Latrines from where excreta are manually removed.
Source: UNWWDR (2003, 113).

between urban and rural dwellers. The UN World Water Development Report (2003) concluded that there was a funding gap of between $110 billion and $180 billion which had to be bridged to achieve the targets.

Conventionally, such funding shortfalls lead to calls for increased international aid. However, over 80% of water infrastructure investment at present comes from domestic (largely public) funding, and it is reasonable to assume that this will continue to be the case. Since about half of those without proper sanitation live in China and India – both with high and sustained rates of economic growth – funding in this case will very likely become available domestically.

There are still, however, countries with about 30% of the world's population that are making little or no progress towards the MDGs for water and sanitation. The great majority of these are in Africa, and there is clearly a case for targeting aid and other forms of external funding towards them.

This money could provide the necessary infrastructure, but past experience shows that this can be poorly correlated with the level of service provided. In many cases, this has been because projects have been donor-driven, top-down, and technology focused, and have failed to involve the local community.

Not only must future projects be community managed, but they must also be integrated. Analysis shows that water supply must be combined with basic sanitation and hygiene awareness campaigns if key health benefits are to be realized. Currently, improved sanitation on average accounts for only about 20% of the total spending on water infrastructure in developing countries, and there is an obvious case for this to be increased.

An economic analysis of a program to meet the MDGs shows the total investment and recurrent costs of sanitation provision as $9.3 billion and that for water supply as $1.8 billion, a total of $11.1 billion. The benefits in terms of sanitation alone amount to over $54 billion: a benefit-cost ratio of nearly 5. Using a 5% discount rate, the project overall has a Net Present Value (NPV) of $400 billion. The major part of the benefit is accounted for by time gained: fewer days off work and school and less time spent nursing sick babies.

Halving the present numbers of people with water and sanitation needs would still leave large numbers unserved: 550 million people without a safe water supply and 1.2 billion with no access to basic sanitation. A simple extrapolation of the costs and benefits of meeting the MDGs suggests that the NPV of providing services to everyone increases to $600 billion. In practice, of course, things are not that simple, and implementing effective water infrastructure projects in countries which are financially unstable or engaged in civil conflict would be extremely difficult.

Opportunity 2: Small-scale water technology for livelihoods

The second option is the exploitation of appropriate low-cost, small-scale technologies that individual farmers can use to improve agricultural productivity. This is applicable to 800 million rural poor people, plus some peri-urban dwellers who depend on farming for a living. To make a real difference, these technologies have to be provided in a supportive environment, where micro-credit, training, and support are available.

Recently, there has been increased focus on the provision of a range of water technologies to smallholders. These include low-cost electric or diesel pumps, a number of manual irrigation systems, and techniques for water harvesting. Such technologies offer a major opportunity to reduce poverty in rural areas.

Drip irrigation is one example of the technologies used. This can give significant yield increases (20–70%) while using less water than traditional methods. Previously the preserve of commercial farmers, the availability of cheap, small-scale equipment has made this an option also for smallholders. For example, the so-called "Pepsee" system in India costs only $93 for equipment to irrigate an acre of cotton. This gives yields almost twice as high as non-adopters, and comparable to those from conventional drip irrigation systems costing twice as much.

Another technology – the manual treadle pump to lift water from ponds and wells – is improving livelihoods in the poorest parts of Southern Asia. Costing only $12–30, these pumps have been found to increase farmers' income by an average of $100 a year. Assuming a typical cost of $20 for a pump, replaced every three years, the Net Present Value for an adopter is $1,900. The total NPV for the $1\frac{1}{2}$ million current users is $2.8 billion, and there are believed to be 10 million potential users in the region in total.

Small-scale rainwater harvesting technologies (to conserve rainfall in the field or by storage) have been actively promoted by NGOs and have been a conspicuous success, particularly in parts of India. In the Gujarat region, tens of thousands of small check dams have already been built. It is estimated that the value of the main monsoon crop across the whole of India could be increased from about $36–54 billion to $180 billion by building two million small check dams at a total cost of $7 billion.

Overall, some 100 million farming families in Asia and Africa could benefit by an average of $100 per year by using small-scale water technology. This yields an NPV of $200 billion in direct benefits. Indirect effects on the overall economy could increase this significantly. Taking the multiplier effect into account, an investment of $100 billion over the MDG timescale would give benefits of $700 billion; a benefit-cost ratio of 7.

Conclusions

The two opportunities discussed above (and the others for which too little information is available to do a proper analysis) rely not just on delivering appropriate technologies, but doing so in an integrated way that focuses on end results. Providing access to clean water and basic sanitation, plus options to improve the productivity of small-scale farming, would have large welfare benefits and help to lift people out of poverty.

THE WATER CHALLENGE
OPPONENTS' VIEWS

Frank Rijsberman's paper on the challenge of water and sanitation provision attracts considerable agreement from the authors of the two opponent papers. John Boland, in particular, is sympathetic to most of the analysis, although he has some doubts about the ease of implementation of the proposals. Henry Vaux, although accepting many of the arguments put forward, has one point of substantial disagreement: He believes that the water challenge is largely defined by scarcity, whereas Rijsberman takes the view that is primarily an issue of fair and effective access.

Vaux agrees with the challenge definition as provision of water and sanitation to the unserved. However, he considers the Millennium Development Goal as an unrealistic basis for quantitative analysis. To halve the numbers of unserved by 2015 implies, for example, bringing sanitation to 825,000 unserved people *each day* from now until 2015. In his words, this does not seem "physically, institutionally, or economically attainable." By extension, the benefits of the proposals would be lower.

He emphasizes the critical point that interventions must be made in combination, and should link appropriate

technology with effective institutions. The neglect of institutional problems has in the past led to the failure of many
schemes. He also concurs with the point that water and sanitation are necessary but not sufficient for economic growth
to occur.

Vaux focuses his discussion on his view that scarcity is
the primary issue that determines the water challenge. This
scarcity is exacerbated by the general assumption that there
are certain fundamental rights to water (a theme which
Boland also takes up). The lack of water, rather than just its
fair distribution, will affect rich and poor alike, and Vaux
sees three key problems:

- Sustainable groundwater. Groundwater accounts for
  about one-third of the world's usable water supply, but
  is threatened by overuse without allowing for regener-
  ation. Water tables are falling virtually everywhere, but
  the problem is particularly serious in China and India.
  This depletion is often addressed by building additional
  surface water storage, but experience shows that this is
  only a temporary respite in the absence of proper controls over extraction.
- Water quality is also a major determinant of availability. Water that is not fit for a particular use is effectively
  unavailable. Although surface water quality in Europe
  and North America has been improving, in other parts
  of the world there has been a continual decline. Unre-
  stricted land use and contamination by natural and syn-
  thetic chemicals are two aspects, and poorer countries
  have the fewest resources to tackle this.

- Agriculture is the major consumer of water, and increasing demands will be made on the supply as the world's population continues to grow. Irrigated agriculture has been criticized, but it is vital for feeding the world and also is a big factor in reducing rural poverty. Undoubtedly irrigation will increase, but there will come a point in water availability (generally about 1,500 cubic metres of water per head per year) below which a country cannot produce all its food needs. The deficit is then made up by imports, effectively shifting the water burden elsewhere. An increased population will therefore intensify water scarcity in countries that currently have a surplus, as well as in those that are already in deficit.

Vaux's conclusion is that the water challenge is even more formidable than Rijsberman suggests in the challenge paper.

John Boland takes a very different approach in his opposition paper. He fully agrees that the water and sanitation problem is a serious one that must be addressed. He sees the costs of poor management as unacceptable, going far beyond economic impacts to encompass significant health impacts, poverty, and major environmental degradation. This makes it important to exploit all promising opportunities, but difficult to evaluate their likely outcome.

A central point to Boland's discussion is the nature of water: whether it is a public good (in which case it should be freely available to all) or a market good (and thus be allocated via normal market forces). He concludes that water supply (as distinct from water in the environment) is a market good. This goes against the opinion of most water planners, who see that "water is different" because it is essential for life.

However, he also argues that the health benefits of universal water access are received not just by individuals but by communities as a whole, and that these benefits constitute a public good. Overall, therefore, his view is that water supply is a market good (and therefore can be supplied privately) but must be subject to public regulation.

He characterizes the two general opportunities proposed by Rijsberman as bottom-up approaches, based on the experience that centralized top-down initiatives have often failed. While acknowledging the sense of this, he also argues for a comprehensive approach using appropriate institutional reform. In his view, the problem is to understand what the barriers are to individual projects and to set up an appropriate program to deal sensitively with these.

Paying for provision of water and sanitation is nearly always socially acceptable, as long as basic provision to the very poorest can be made at little or no cost. However, tariffs need to be designed sensitively, and there is no "one size fits all" solution.

In Boland's view, a major problem is how to predict the degree of successful implementation. Given that many of the easier projects have probably already been taken up, future extensions may well be more difficult. It is probably unrealistic to expect all goals to be fully achieved, but even falling short by a large margin would yield enormous benefits. With many of the projects, there are no economies of scale, so projects could be implemented selectively on the basis of a fuller assessment, giving even higher benefit-cost ratios in individual cases.

In summary, Boland believes the identified opportunities are manifestly worthwhile, but thinks their goals should be more realistic.

9 Subsidies and Trade Barriers

The challenge

Eliminating government subsidies and trade barriers has clear economic benefits. Despite evidence that those policies harm the economies that impose them, and are particularly harmful to the world's poor, governments continue to intervene in markets for both goods and services. This chapter argues that phasing out these trade-distorting policies should be the highest priority among the opportunities assessed. Not only would this strategy have a direct effect on poverty reduction, but there would also be indirect benefits across the full range of Copenhagen Consensus challenges. Moreover, the relatively small costs of adjustment to reform would leave plenty of the notional $50 billion to be spent on second priorities.

The most recent big surge of protectionism was about 75 years ago. Following the Second World War, governments of major industrial countries – well aware of the economic rationale for free trade – sought ways to reduce import tariffs. But politicians fear making changes that may be associated with politically unpopular redistributions of jobs, income, and wealth. The challenge therefore involves finding politically attractive ways to phase out the remaining distortions in world markets for goods, services, capital, and, potentially, even labor.

The arguments for and against removing subsidies and trade barriers

Free trade is often criticized by non-economists on the assumption that it has negative social and environmental consequences, as evidenced by the burgeoning "antiglobalization" movements. But these need to be weighed against various positive social and environmental consequences as well as the net economic benefits – both static and dynamic – of meeting the challenge.

Static gains arise from countries producing more of the goods and services they can provide most efficiently, and less of what others can produce more efficiently. Each country will maximize the value of its output of goods or services and these will be sought by trading partners because they are competitively priced. After trading, each individual country will be better off than in a world without trade. This is commonly referred to as the principle of comparative advantage. The smaller the economy, the greater the static gains from trade tend to be as a share of national output.

Additionally, *dynamic* gains result as increased trade fuels economic growth. Typically, freeing up imports of intermediates and capital goods encourages entrepreneurs to make greater investments in production capacity. Evidence gathered during the second half of the twentieth century shows that countries that have liberalized their trade have enjoyed an average 1.5% increase in annual GDP growth compared with the pre-reform rate. Of course, governments also need to do other things right to attract investment, such as protecting property rights and maintaining financial and political stability. Free trade is a necessary, but not sufficient, condition for sustained economic growth.

Despite the potential gains from trade, most governments retain at least some protectionist policies. The reason is political. Although the total wealth of an economy increases when trade is liberalized, owners of capital and workers in the most protected industries may lose, and any compensation typically covers only a small fraction of those losses. The losses are concentrated in the hands of relatively few people who are prepared to lobby the government and support protection-minded politicians, whereas the benefits are spread widely across industries and the general population such that the recipients face a free-rider problem in banding together to lobby for reform.

Governments are also influenced by the arguments of NGOs who claim globalization is adding to social and environmental problems in both rich and poor countries, despite evidence to the contrary.

There are, however, a number of ways in which trade reform can be fostered or initiated, including:

- Better dissemination of the case for free trade by governments, think tanks, and those directly involved in import and export, to counter lobbying by NGOs, trade unions, and other special-interest groups.

- Technological changes – for example, the revolution in information and communications in the last two decades – that can dramatically lower the costs of doing business internationally.
- Unilateral liberalization by other countries, which can highlight the benefits of open markets.
- Opportunities to join international trade agreements, which can provide more politically acceptable alternatives to unilateral liberalization (although bilateral and regional deals have less potential to add to national and global welfare than broader multilateral trade agreements).

The opportunities

There are four opportunities considered here:

- **Opportunity 1** is to move to a world free from subsidies and trade barriers: free trade in its purest form. Although this seems politically unlikely at present, it gives a benchmark against which other options can be measured.
- **Opportunity 2** is to successfully complete the current round of WTO negotiations: the Doha development agenda. This would involve a global legally binding partial trade liberalization, with all participants on an equal footing, as WTO members account for more than 95 percent of global trade. Success is far from assured,

however, and the timeline for its completion is likely to extend significantly beyond the current deadline of the end of 2004 unless extraordinary efforts are made by the major players.

- **Opportunity 3** comprises a range of more limited, but nonetheless important, regional trade agreements, for example via the Asia Pacific Economic Cooperation (APEC) forum or European Union (EU) enlargement. The APEC agreement is non-binding but also non-preferential – it gives market access to all trading partners of each signatory (a so-called 'Most Favored Nation' or MFN reform) and is thus effectively a subset of WTO reforms. EU expansion is an example of a reciprocal preferential agreement: All participants have access to each other's markets, but their external trading partners are excluded from the deal. Following the EU's expansion eastward in May 2004, the most ambitious reciprocal preferential agreement in prospect is the proposed Free Trade Area of the Americas (FTAA), which would bring together all the economies of North, Central, and South America, so it is this agreement which is considered here.

- **Opportunity 4** covers agreements that enable preferential market access for exports from developing countries to rich economies: so called non-reciprocal preferential trade agreements. EU countries have allowed imports from former colonies on this basis in the past, but the EU proposal to provide duty- and quota-free access for all least-developed countries is being embraced by numerous advanced industrial economies.

Benefits and costs of reducing subsidies and trade barriers

Economic benefits

Most published studies reviewed in this chapter employ computer simulation models of the global economy of the computable general equilibrium (CGE) type. These have increasingly been used for analysis of multilateral trade reform since their introduction in the late 1970s. Although by no means perfect (after all, they are only models), they capture the economy-wide nature of adjustments and yet include sufficient detail of industrial sectors to be useful to a wide range of parties.

These models have been used by trade economists most commonly to analyze the effects of reducing trade barriers and agricultural production and export subsidies. Non-agricultural subsidies are not considered because they are not the main focus of WTO negotiations, precise data on them are at best patchy, and, in any case, agricultural subsidies are estimated to account for some 40% of all government subsidies.

Opportunity 1 – Removing all trade barriers and agricultural subsidies

Relatively few studies have considered this most radical option. The benefits derived vary with assumptions, ranging from $254 billion per year from 2005 (with $108 billion of this accruing to developing countries) to $2,080 billion (with $431 billion to developing countries). The higher figure assumes also liberalization of services, including foreign direct investment. Three other studies give benefit figures falling between these two extremes.

All of the studies show agriculture to be the main contributor to gains, accounting for 65–70% of the total. This reflects the high degree of protection from farm imports in nearly all countries (both rich and poor) and the direct government support of farming in some rich countries.

None of the studies examine the effect of freeing completely the international movement of labor. However, it was recently estimated that even a modest relaxation – allowing temporary immigration to increase industrialized country labor forces by just 3% (which would involve 16.4 million workers from developing countries) – would increase global income by $156 billion. Most of the benefit would accrue to the developing country migrants.

Opportunity 2 – Reducing trade barriers and agricultural subsidies in the WTO's Doha round

This so-called "development" round of trade negotiations, which started in November 2001, has made intermittent progress to date. We can nonetheless consider the potential benefits.

An optimistic assumption of 50% across-the-board cuts to bound tariffs and farm subsidies leads to predicted benefits of approximately half those to be derived from full liberalization – around $200 to $1,000 billion a year – although with a different balance of beneficiaries. No allowance has been made in those estimates for reform-stimulated economic growth or for the effect of liberalizing labor or capital markets. If these were included, the benefit could be much higher.

Opportunity 3 – Removing intra-American trade barriers following the FTAA negotiations

The creation of regional Free Trade Areas (FTAs) – even one as large as the proposed Free Trade Area of the Americas (FTAA) – has limited benefits. The gains would be a small fraction of those to be derived from a significant liberalization of world trade via the WTO. No doubt some individual developing countries would benefit, but no more so than if global trade barriers were modestly reduced.

There is also a downside to such areas: Some countries benefit by being in the FTA, but this can be at the expense of excluded economies. The net global effect could even be negative, with greater losses from trade diversions from excluded countries than gains by FTA members. Nevertheless, agreements of this type continue to be pursued, not least because they can be brought about faster and with less political difficulty than multilateral changes via the WTO.

Opportunity 4 – Removing developed country barriers to exports from least-developed countries

An example of this approach is the EU's proposal to extend to United Nations-designated "least developed countries" (LDCs) duty- and quota-free access for exports of "everything but arms" (EBA). This may sound like a good idea, but it does not include trade in services, particularly the right for LDC workers to obtain temporary work permits, and has a number of other drawbacks.

Necessarily this initiative is tiny in terms of global impact, because LDCs are such a small part of the global economy. Certainly it could have significant benefits for some people in sub-Saharan Africa (SSA), where exports could increase by perhaps $0.5 billion a year, according to World Bank estimates. A wider World Bank study suggests that LDCs across the world could benefit by up to $2.5 billion if they had unfettered access for their exports to the EU, the USA, Canada, and Japan. However, this would be partly at the expense of other, not necessarily poorer, developing countries. Also, it would give LDCs little incentive to reduce their own internal and external barriers to trade, and would eliminate their incentive to push for global trade liberalization at the WTO.

How can progress best be made by 2010?

If progress is to be made in the face of strong protectionist pressure from powerful domestic interest groups, a multi-pronged approach must be adopted. This would encourage both unilateral reform within countries and comprehensive multilateral reform through the WTO, supplemented by regional initiatives of the sort which support both. To counter the entrenched protectionist forces whose lobbying of national governments is extremely influential, the case for free trade needs to be made more strongly, for

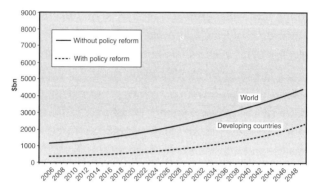

Figure 9.1. Annual increment to global GDP without and with 50 per cent cut to subsidies and trade barriers, 2006–2050 ($US 2002 bn)

example by sponsoring policy think tanks and others able to effectively disseminate to the gainers from trade reform the empirical findings of researchers.

Preferential trade agreements seem destined to be part of the ongoing move toward liberalization, although on their own they are not the best solution. Non-reciprocal agreements (Opportunity 4) in particular are of doubtful value, discouraging further liberalization and disadvantaging non-LDC developing countries (which include such poor countries as Vietnam). Free Trade Areas have similar drawbacks, and deliver only a fraction of the benefits realizable from WTO-based multilateral reform.

Summary of gross benefits

As a working figure, an average of the upper and lower bounds of studies used as a basis for this chapter has been taken: This amounts to a 1.8% increase in global GDP as the static gain (that is, taking no account of reform-stimulated economic growth) after full adjustment to the new regime. For developing countries, the benefits would be relatively higher: 2.5% of GDP. It is assumed that the gains will begin at one-fifth of that rate but rise by one-fifth each year from 2006 until 2010 when they are assumed to be fully realized.

In addition, there are dynamic gains from free trade. A conservative estimate is that reform would boost the annual rate of economic growth by one-sixth for developed countries and one-third for developing countries. For the world as a whole, growth would rise from 3.2% to 3.8% a year, while for developing countries this would raise their average annual growth rate from 4.6% to 6.1%. To again err on the conservative side, this higher rate of growth is assumed to continue just until 2050 rather than forever.

Economic costs

The costs incurred in the reform process are one-off, in contrast to the gains which are long-term and continuing. Costs include those associated with negotiation rounds, support for policy think tanks, adjustments for companies and workers, and social costs and welfare payments for the temporarily unemployed. Studies tend to show that such costs are relatively small compared to the gains, and are minimized by careful phasing in of reforms. However, governments may still be reluctant to reform since job losses tend to be concentrated and highly visible, whereas the gains are spread so thinly across the entire economy as to not be obvious to most citizens.

For the purposes of this chapter, it is assumed that the adjustment period following 50% liberalization lasts for five years (considerably longer than has been found in most case studies). For each year, the cost is assumed to be one-third of the eventual total static benefit of the reform: $243 billion annually for the period 2006–2010, with $71 billion of that incurred in developing countries.

Social and environmental benefits

By generating large economic gains over a long period, trade reform would indirectly help to tackle the other global challenges by making more funds available. However, there would also be direct effects on a number of key challenges. For example:

- *Poverty reduction* would be fostered, as faster-growing developing economies have been shown to be better at reducing poverty than countries with slow economic growth.
- *Communicable diseases* could be tackled more effectively by countries where poverty is reduced and medicines are more widely available and affordable.
- *Conflicts* are likely to be reduced when countries are more economically interdependent and where there are fewer barriers to migration.
- *Educational under-investment* particularly by poor families in developing countries is likely to be alleviated by trade reform-induced increases in international prices for farm and textile products.

Global benefit-cost ratios

Lower-bound estimates for the overall net benefits of halving subsidies and trade barriers indicate an approximate doubling of annual GDP growth after the initial (assumed five year) adjustment period. Assuming there were no further benefits after 2050 (though this is unlikely) and using a discount rate of 5%, the net present value would be $23 trillion for the world economy, with half of this accruing to the current developing economies. Given the present value of estimated adjustment etc. and so on costs of just under $1 trillion, the benefit-cost ratio is 24.3 globally, and 37.9 for the developing countries.

If social and environmental benefits and costs were included, these figures would most likely be considerably higher. Even if more conservative assumptions are made about the success of the Doha round and the transition period, benefits are still likely to be enormous and the costs easily justifiable. All this is within our grasp, given bold leadership and a willingness to make the most of the opportunity available for unilateral and multilateral trade reform, particularly within the WTO framework.

SUBSIDIES AND TRADE BARRIERS

In his challenge paper, Kym Anderson makes a strong case for maximum liberalization of trade, not only as a good in itself, but also as a way to contribute to the other high-priority challenges. Both opponents agree that free trade has economic benefits, but have concerns about how these might best be generated and shared.

Arvind Panagariya whole heartedly supports Anderson's case for trade liberalization to be the highest priority among the challenges and, indeed, considers it essential if all the others are to be met. Nevertheless, he has some critical points to make. In particular, he thinks that the case would be stronger if more details were given of the nature and size of some of the barriers. Also, benefits are not uniformly distributed: The impact on some developing countries would actually be negative.

Anderson makes the case for liberalization on the basis of broad generalizations, where cause (liberalization) inevitably leads to the desired effect (increased growth). In Panagariya's view, this relationship cannot be guaranteed, and he sees openness instead as being necessary, but not sufficient, for sustained rapid growth.

Looking at the first of Anderson's identified opportunities – unilateral liberalization – Panagariya sees ample evidence for the benefits of this, citing in particular the dramatic improvements in growth resulting from India and China following such a path. To critics who point to the disastrous experiences of Latin American countries in the 1980s and '90s, he argues that the root cause was not excessive liberalization but macroeconomic instability leading to excessive foreign borrowing (itself a problem considered as a separate challenge). Chile represents a unique success story in the region at that time because it followed prudent domestic economic policies while slashing subsidies.

Multilateral liberalization via completion of the Doha round of World Trade Organisation (WTO) negotiations is the second opportunity, also supported by Panagariya. Given the complexity of the negotiations, he thinks that halving of barriers by 2010 is unrealistic; however *agreement* to the elimination of industrial tariffs by a later date is quite feasible. On the question of agriculture, he makes the point that removal of subsidies would actually harm the majority of developing countries, which are net food importers and would thus suffer from higher prices. Ironically, it would be richer countries (the USA in particular) that would gain most, even though it is their subsidies which would be cut.

Safety nets and transitional arrangements will be needed to protect the developing countries that would be disadvantaged in the short term. However, this negative impact must be recognized and acknowledged by the rest of the world before such policies could be put in place.

Panagariya agrees with Anderson that the introduction of more Free Trade Areas and one-way preferential trading arrangements between poor and rich countries have little to offer in terms of increased growth. There are few success stories, the maze of agreements complicates trade, and little incentive is left for multilateral reform that would be of greater benefit. He is also concerned that such agreements come with strings attached, such as commitment to American views on intellectual property rights.

In his opposition notes, Jan Pronk raises many of the same points, but expresses particular concerns about the negative implications for some countries and social groups. He believes in the value of free trade, but argues for a greater integration with domestic political policy making to maximize the benefits. He also does not see a direct role for free trade in meeting the other challenges; to him trade is only one of a number of important factors.

Pronk, by arguing for a more balanced evaluation of the opportunities for free trade with other aspects of a domestic political agenda (such as education, research, the environment, and social welfare policies) is offering a broader, more politically focused view of Panagariya's point that trade liberalization is a necessary but not sufficient factor for sustained growth. In Pronk's view, the ultimate objective of economic policy making is not to expand trade but to increase income and welfare.

Expanding on this, he points out that countries need good institutions and economic and political stability to benefit from free trade. He argues also for a gradualist approach to opening markets: China has experienced sustained rapid growth, partly at the expense of the environment and a sound banking system. The European Union, on the other hand, has taken a long time to liberalize, not because politicians did not recognize the benefits, but because they feared the social consequences of less considered action. So, despite the distortions of the Common Agricultural Policy, European farmers are in a better position than in many other countries.

Pronk is sceptical about Anderson's proposal to lessen resistance to free trade by providing more pro-market information. In his view, many citizens see subsidies as a way of promoting political and social stability, whatever the economic arguments for cutting them. Politicians will proceed cautiously to avoid creating greater inequalities. In this context, he agrees that a combination of unilateral reform at national level with multilateral action through the WTO is both sensible and politically feasible.

Although the benefits of liberalization are great and Anderson's estimates are indeed conservative, that does not mean they will be easy to bring about. This is because the benefits are unequally distributed (to date favoring rich countries) and the structural and social costs are both greater and longer term than accounted for in the challenge paper. Inequalities have been widening as trade restrictions have loosened; Pronk is therefore doubtful that free trade will do much to directly reduce poverty. Neither does he necessarily see a positive effect on the environment.

In summary, both opponents agree that trade liberalization could bring great economic benefits, but argue that reform has to be combined with other important aspects of policy if success is to be achieved.

Expert Panel Ranking

PANEL: JAGDISH N. BHAGWATI, ROBERT W. FOGEL,
BRUNO S. FREY, JUSTIN YIFU LIN, DOUGLASS C. NORTH,
THOMAS C. SCHELLING, VERNON L. SMITH, NANCY L. STOKEY

The goal of the project

The goal of the Copenhagen Consensus project was to set priorities among a series of proposals for confronting 10 great global challenges. These challenges, selected from a wider set of issues identified by the United Nations, were: climate change; communicable diseases; conflicts and arms proliferation; access to education; financial instability; governance and corruption; malnutrition and hunger; migration; sanitation and access to clean water; and subsidies and trade barriers.

A panel of economic experts, comprising eight of the world's most distinguished economists, was invited to consider these issues. The members were Jagdish N. Bhagwati of Columbia University, Robert S. Fogel of the University of Chicago (Nobel Laureate), Bruno W. Frey of the University of Zurich, Justin Yifu Lin of Peking University, Douglass C. North of Washington University in St Louis (Nobel Laureate), Thomas C. Schelling of the University of Maryland, Vernon L. Smith of George Mason University (Nobel Laureate), and Nancy L. Stokey of the University of Chicago.

The panel was asked to address the 10 challenge areas and to answer the question: "What would be the best ways of advancing global welfare, and particularly the welfare of developing countries, supposing that an additional $50 billion of resources were at governments' disposal?" Ten challenge papers, commissioned from acknowledged authorities in each area of policy, set out more than thirty proposals for the panel's consideration. During the conference, the panel examined these proposals in detail. Each chapter was discussed at length with its principal author and with two other specialists who had been commissioned to write critical appraisals in the form of Perspective papers, and then the experts met in private session. Finally, the panel ranked the proposals in descending order of desirability (see following table).

CHALLENGE	OPPORTUNITY
VERY GOOD	
1 Communicable diseases	Control of HIV/AIDS
2 Malnutrition and hunger	Providing micronutrients
3 Subsidies and trade barriers	Trade liberalization
4 Communicable diseases	Control of malaria
GOOD	
5 Malnutrition and hunger	Development of new agricultural technologies
6 Sanitation and water	Small-scale water technology for livelihoods
7 Sanitation and water	Community-managed water supply and sanitation
8 Sanitation and water	Research on water productivity in food production

CHALLENGE	OPPORTUNITY
9 Governance and corruption	Lowering the cost of starting a new business
FAIR	
10 Migration	Lowering barriers to migration for skilled workers
11 Malnutrition and hunger	Improving infant and child nutrition
12 Communicable diseases	Scaled-up basic health services
13 Malnutrition and hunger	Reducing the prevalence of Low Birth Weight
BAD	
14 Migration	Guest-worker programs for the unskilled
15 Climate change	Optimal carbon tax
16 Climate change	The Kyoto Protocol
17 Climate change	Value-at-risk carbon tax

Ranking the proposals

In ordering the proposals, the panel was guided predominantly by consideration of *economic costs and benefits*. The panel acknowledged the difficulties that cost-benefit analysis (CBA) must overcome, both in principle and as a practical matter, but agreed that CBA was an indispensable organizing method. In setting priorities, the panel took account of the strengths and weaknesses of the specific cost-benefit appraisals under review, and gave weight both to the institutional preconditions for success and to the demands of ethical or humanitarian urgency. As a general matter, the panel noted that higher standards of governance and improvements in the institutions required to support development in the world's poor countries were of paramount importance.

Some of the proposals (for instance, the lowering of barriers to trade or migration) face political resistance. Overcoming such resistance can be regarded as a "cost" of implementation. The panel took the view that such political costs should be excluded from their calculations: They concerned themselves only with those *economic costs of delivery*, including the costs of specific supporting institutional reforms, which would be faced once the political decision to proceed had been taken.

For some of the proposals, the panel found that information was too sparse to permit a judgement to be made. These proposals, some of which may prove, after further study, to be valuable, were therefore excluded from the ranking.

Each expert assigned his or her own ranking to the proposals. The individual rankings, together with commentaries prepared by each expert, will be published in due course. (The chapters and other material have already been placed in the public domain.) The panel's ranking was calculated by taking the median of individual rankings. The panel jointly endorses the median ordering shown above as representing their agreed view.

Communicable diseases

The panel ranked at 1 new measures to prevent the spread of HIV/AIDS. Spending assigned to this purpose would yield extraordinarily high benefits, averting nearly 30 million new infections by 2010. Costs are substantial, estimated at $27 billion. Even so, these costs are small in relation to what stands to be gained. Moreover, the scale and urgency of the problem – especially in Africa, where AIDS threatens the collapse of entire societies – are extreme.

New measures for the control and treatment of malaria were jointly ranked at 4. At $13 billion in costs, the benefit-cost ratio (BCR) was somewhat lower than for the proposals on HIV/AIDS and malnutrition and hunger, but still extremely high by the ordinary standards of project appraisal, especially for the provision of chemically treated bednets (ITNs). Again, the scale and urgency of the problem are very great. Scaled-up basic health services were ranked at 12.

Malnutrition and hunger

Policies to attack malnutrition and hunger were ranked at 2. Reducing the prevalence of iron-deficiency anaemia by means of food supplements, in particular, has an exceptionally high BCR; of the three proposals considered under this heading, this was ranked highest at $12 billion. The expert panel ranked a second proposal, to increase spending on research into new agricultural technologies appropriate for poor countries, at 5. Further proposals, for additional spending on infant and child nutrition and on reducing the prevalence of LBW, were ranked at 11 and 13, respectively.

Global trade reform

The panel considered three main proposals for global trade reform: first, multilateral and unilateral reduction of tariffs and non-tariff barriers (NTBs), together with the elimination of agricultural subsidies; second, extension of regional trade agreements (RTAs); third, adoption of the 'Everything But Arms' (EBA) proposal for non-reciprocal lowering of rich-country tariffs on exports from the least developed countries (LDCs). In the case of trade reform, lives are not directly and immediately at risk. However, the first proposal – free trade – was agreed to yield exceptionally large benefits, in relation to comparatively modest adjustment costs, both for the world as a whole and for the developing countries. Accordingly it was ranked at 3. (Some members of the panel argued that since this proposal need not involve any budgetary outlays, it should be acted upon in any case, regardless of the resources available for additional budget outlays.) The proposal to extend regional free trade areas (FTAs) was not ranked, for lack of information on particular agreements. The proposal for non-reciprocal lowering of barriers to exports of the LDCs was also not ranked, with some members of the panel noting that this proposal would harm many poor countries not participating in the arrangements, and encourage those that did participate to invest in activities that were not internationally competitive.

Sanitation and access to clean water

The panel agreed with Chapter 8 on sanitation and access to clean water that the lack of safe and affordable access to these services is a great burden for more than a billion of the world's poorest people. Almost half of the people living in developing countries suffer at any given time from one or more water-borne diseases. Three proposals, including small-scale water technology for livelihoods, were regarded as likely to be highly cost-effective and were ranked at 6, 7, and 8.

Governance and corruption

The experts considered five proposals for improving governance in developing countries. Although agreeing, as already noted, that better governance is very often a precondition for progress of any kind, the panel thought it inappropriate to include four of these proposals in their ranking. This is because these reforms involve costs of implementation that will differ greatly according to each country's particular institutional circumstances. The experts felt they had too little specific information to make a judgement about what those costs might be. The panel did, however, express its support for the proposal to reduce the state-imposed costs of starting a new business, on the grounds that this policy would not only be enormously beneficial but also relatively straightforward to introduce. This proposal was ranked at 9.

Migration

Policies to liberalize international migration were regarded as a desirable way to promote global welfare and to provide economic opportunities to people in developing countries. A lowering of barriers to the migration of skilled workers was recommended, and ranked at 10. Guest-worker programs, of the sort common in Europe, were not recommended, owing to their tendency to discourage the assimilation of migrants.

Climate change

The panel looked at three proposals, including the Kyoto Protocol, for dealing with climate change by reducing emissions of carbon. The expert panel regarded all three proposals as having costs that were likely to exceed the benefits. The panel recognized that global warming must be addressed, but agreed that approaches based on too abrupt a shift toward lower emissions of carbon were needlessly expensive. The experts expressed an interest in an alternative, proposed in Mendelsohn's perspective opposition paper, which envisaged a carbon tax much lower in the first years of implementation than the figures called for in Clinés paper and Chapter 1 rising gradually in later years. Such a proposal, however, was not examined in detail in the presentations put to the panel, and so was not ranked. The panel urged increased funding for research into more affordable carbon-abatement technologies.

Access to education

The panel considered proposals to improve the provision of education in developing countries. It agreed that in countries where spending on education at present is very low, the potential exists for large benefits in return for modestly increased spending. However, the institutional preconditions for success are demanding and vary from case to case:

Experience suggests that it is easy to waste large sums on education initiatives. Given this variety of circumstances and constraints, the panel chose not to rank any proposals in this area. However, the experts did endorse the view that externally supervised examinations improved accountability of schools and should be promoted. They also expressed an interest in schemes to reduce, in a targeted way, the fees charged in many developing countries for public education, and to pay grants to families that send their children to school. More research on experience with such schemes is needed.

Conflicts

In considering a series of proposals for reducing the incidence of civil wars, the panel unanimously agreed with Chapter 3's assessment that the human and economic costs of such conflicts are enormous – even larger, in fact, than is generally assumed. Measures to reduce the number, duration, or severity of civil wars would stand very high in the ordering, if they could be expected with any confidence to succeed. Members of the panel were not persuaded that the proposals put before them met that test. The panel noted the strong *prima facie* case for additional financial support for regional peacekeeping forces in post-conflict countries that meet certain criteria, but felt that the information before them was insufficient for them to assign a ranking. The experts also noted the evidence that growth in incomes reduced the long-term incidence of civil war; to the extent that should their highest ranked proposals raised incomes, they would have the additional benefit of reducing the incidence of conflict.

Financial instability

Four proposals before the panel addressed the issue of international financial instability. The panel, noting the complexities and uncertainties in this area, chose not to come to a view about which, if any, of these proposals to recommend. They were therefore not ranked.

Index